The Perfect

Slow Cooker

Cookbook for Beginners

1800+ Easy, Yummy Slow Cooker Recipe Book to Save Cooking Time for Busy Families and Eat Healthy Every Day | Any Occasion

Helen J. Blanton

No need to supervise the finished cooking

Setup and go, so easy

Ingredients within reach of local markets

Detailed step-by-step instructions and cooking times

Comprehensive cooking guide for any level

CONTENTS

INTRODUCTION

Allow me to invite you into the world of slow cooking through the pages of Helen J. Blanton's Slow Cooker Cookbook. With a culinary journey that spans my career as a seasoned chef, I've meticulously crafted this cookbook with a deep-rooted passion for creating both convenience and culinary excellence.

My mission is twofold: to democratize the art of slow cooking and to transform ordinary ingredients into extraordinary dishes. This cookbook isn't just a compilation of recipes; it's a culinary companion designed to elevate your cooking experience.

What truly sets it apart is a commitment to your culinary success. Every recipe is carefully curated with step-by-step instructions to guarantee flawless outcomes every time. For those with a penchant for culinary creativity, you'll discover Bonus DIY recipe pages, shopping lists for efficient grocery trips, estimated cooking times to suit your busy life, and practical tips honed from years of slow-cooking exploration.

Whether you're new to the world of slow cooking or a seasoned pro, my aspiration is to make your culinary journey not only flavorsome but also hassle-free and memorable. Together, let's embark on a vibrant adventure, explore the boundless possibilities of the slow cooker, and relish the joy of crafting extraordinary meals for your cherished ones.

What is Slow Cooker?

A Slow Cooker, often referred to as a Crock Pot (a popular brand of slow cooker), is a countertop kitchen appliance used for convenient and low-effort cooking. It's designed for slow, gradual cooking at low temperatures over an extended period, typically several hours. The main components of a slow cooker include a heating element, a ceramic or metal cooking pot (often removable), and a glass or plastic lid. Slow cookers are popular for preparing stews, soups, roasts, and other one-pot meals. They are known for their "set it and forget it" convenience, as you can place your ingredients in the cooker, set the temperature and cooking time, and allow it to simmer and develop flavors while you go about your day. Slow cookers are valued for their ability to tenderize tough cuts of meat and infuse dishes with rich, hearty flavors.

Who is Slow Cooker suitable for?

Busy Professionals: For those with hectic schedules, a slow cooker is a time-saving solution that allows them to come home to a hot, freshly cooked meal.

Families: Ideal for families with multiple members, as it can accommodate larger portion sizes and offers a convenient way to prepare meals for everyone.

Singles and Couples: Even smaller households can benefit from slow cookers, as they allow for cooking in smaller quantities with the option of leftovers.

Seniors: A slow cooker is a safe and easy-to-use appliance that reduces the need for extended periods of standing and monitoring on the stovetop.

Home Cooks: Culinary enthusiasts can experiment with a variety of recipes and cooking techniques in a slow cooker, from stews and roasts to desserts and more.

Meal Preppers: Those who like to prepare meals in advance for the week can utilize the slow cooker for efficient batch cooking.

Budget-Conscious Individuals: Slow cookers are cost-effective, as they often use less expensive cuts of meat and allow for economical meal planning.

Tips for using Slow Cooker

● **Choose the Right Cut of Meat**

Slow cooking is perfect for tough cuts of meat like chuck roast, pork shoulder, or brisket. The long cooking time breaks down the collagen, resulting in tender, flavorful meat. Trim excess fat before cooking to avoid overly greasy dishes.

● **Layer Ingredients Wisely**

Proper layering is essential for even cooking. Place dense, slow-cooking vegetables like potatoes and carrots at the bottom, followed by the meat, and top with quicker-cooking ingredients like mushrooms and bell peppers. This arrangement ensures everything cooks evenly.

● **Don't Lift the Lid Too Often**

It's tempting to check on your meal, but each time you lift the lid, heat and moisture escape, which can significantly increase cooking time. Only open the lid if the recipe requires stirring or adding ingredients.

● **Use the Right Amount of Liquid**

Slow cookers require less liquid than traditional cooking methods. Use just enough to cover the ingredients, as the sealed environment prevents evaporation. Too much liquid can result in a watery dish.

● **Adjust Seasoning and Herbs**

Herbs and spices can lose potency during long cooking times. To maximize flavor, add fresh herbs and spices toward the end of the cooking process. Taste the dish before serving and adjust seasoning as needed.

Breakfast Recipes

Breakfast Recipes

Creamy Yogurt

Servings: 8

Cooking Time: 10 Hours

Ingredients:

- 3 teaspoons gelatin
- ½ gallon milk
- 7 ounces plain yogurt
- 1 and ½ tablespoons vanilla extract
- ½ cup maple syrup

Directions:

1. Put the milk in your Crock Pot, cover and cook on Low for 3 hours.
2. In a bowl, mix 1 cup of hot milk from the Crock Pot with the gelatin, whisk well, pour into the Crock Pot, cover and leave aside for 2 hours.
3. Combine 1 cup of milk with the yogurt, whisk really well and pour into the pot.
4. Also add vanilla and maple syrup, stir, cover and cook on Low for 7 more hours.
5. Leave yogurt aside to cool down and serve it for breakfast.

Nutrition Info:

- calories 200, fat 4, fiber 5, carbs 10, protein 5

Tomato Eggs

Servings:4

Cooking Time: 2.5 Hours

Ingredients:

- 2 cups tomatoes, chopped
- ¼ cup tomato juice
- 1 onion, diced
- 1 teaspoon olive oil
- ½ teaspoon ground black pepper
- 4 eggs

Directions:

1. Pour olive oil in the Crock Pot.
2. Add onion, tomato juice, and tomatoes.
3. Close the lid and cook the mixture on High for 1 hour.
4. Then mix the tomato mixture and crack the eggs inside.
5. Close the lid and cook them on High for 1.5 hours more.

Nutrition Info:

- Per Serving: 103 calories, 6.8g protein, 7.2g carbohydrates, 5.8g fat, 1.8g fiber, 164mg cholesterol, 108mg sodium, 350mg potassium

Squash Bowls

Servings: 2

Cooking Time: 6 Hours

Ingredients:

- 2 tablespoons walnuts, chopped
- 2 cups squash, peeled and cubed
- ½ cup coconut cream
- ½ teaspoon cinnamon powder
- ½ tablespoon sugar

Directions:

1. In your Crock Pot, mix the squash with the nuts and the other ingredients, toss, put the lid on and cook on Low for 6 hours.
2. Divide into bowls and serve.

Nutrition Info:

- calories 140, fat 1, fiber 2, carbs 2, protein 5

Broccoli Egg Casserole

Servings:5

Cooking Time: 3 Hours

Ingredients:

- 4 eggs, beaten
- ½ cup full-fat milk
- 3 tablespoons grass-fed butter, melted
- 1 ½ cup broccoli florets, chopped
- Salt and pepper to taste

Directions:

1. Beat the eggs and milk in a mixing bowl.
2. Grease the bottom of the CrockPot with melted butter.
3. Add in the broccoli florets in the CrockPot and pour the egg mixture.
4. Season with salt and pepper to taste.
5. Close the lid and cook on high for 2 hours or on low for 3 hours.

Nutrition Info:

- Calories per serving: 217; Carbohydrates:4.6 g; Protein: 11.6g; Fat: 16.5g; Sugar: 0.7g; Sodium: 674mg; Fiber: 2.3g

Chocolate Toast

Servings:4

Cooking Time:40 Minutes

Ingredients:

- 4 white bread slices
- 1 tablespoon vanilla extract
- 2 tablespoons Nutella
- 1 banana, mashed
- 1 tablespoon coconut oil
- ¼ cup full-fat milk

Directions:

1. Mix vanilla extract, Nutella, mashed banana, coconut oil, and milk.
2. Pour the mixture in the Crock Pot and cook on High for 40 minutes.
3. Make a quick pressure release and cool the chocolate mixture.
4. Spread the toasts with cooked mixture.

Nutrition Info:

- Per Serving: 148 calories, 2g protein, 18.2g carbohydrates, 7.1g fat, 1.5g fiber, 2mg cholesterol, 73mg sodium, 182mg potassium.

Cauliflower Rice Pudding

Servings: 2

Cooking Time: 2 Hours

Ingredients:

- ¼ cup maple syrup
- 3 cups almond milk
- 1 cup cauliflower rice
- 2 tablespoons vanilla extract

Directions:

1. Put cauliflower rice in your Crock Pot, add maple syrup, almond milk and vanilla extract, stir, cover and cook on High for 2 hours.
2. Stir your pudding again, divide into bowls and serve for breakfast.

Nutrition Info:

- calories 240, fat 2, fiber 2, carbs 15, protein 5

Brussels Sprouts Omelet

Servings: 4

Cooking Time: 4 Hours

Ingredients:

- 4 eggs, whisked
- Salt and black pepper to the taste
- 1 tablespoon olive oil
- 2 green onions, minced
- 2 garlic cloves, minced
- 12 ounces Brussels sprouts, sliced
- 2 ounces bacon, chopped

Directions:

1. Drizzle the oil on the bottom of your Crock Pot and spread Brussels sprouts, garlic, bacon, green onions, eggs, salt and pepper, toss, cover and cook on Low for 4 hours.
2. Divide between plates and serve right away for breakfast.

Nutrition Info:

- calories 240, fat 7, fiber 4, carbs 7, protein 13

Cranberry Quinoa

Servings: 4

Cooking Time: 2 Hours

Ingredients:

- 3 cups coconut water
- 1 teaspoon vanilla extract
- 1 cup quinoa
- 3 teaspoons honey
- 1/8 cup almonds, sliced
- 1/8 cup coconut flakes
- ¼ cup cranberries, dried

Directions:

1. In your Crock Pot, mix coconut water with vanilla, quinoa, honey, almonds, coconut flakes and cranberries, toss, cover and cook on High for 2 hours.
2. Divide quinoa mix into bowls and serve.

Nutrition Info:

- calories 261, fat 7, fiber 8, carbs 18, protein

Beef Meatloaf

Servings: 2

Cooking Time: 4 Hours

Ingredients:

- 1 red onion, chopped
- 1 pound beef stew meat, ground
- ½ teaspoon chili powder
- 1 egg, whisked
- ½ teaspoon olive oil
- ½ teaspoon sweet paprika
- 2 tablespoons white flour
- ½ teaspoon oregano, chopped
- ½ tablespoon basil, chopped
- A pinch of salt and black pepper
- ½ teaspoon marjoram, dried

Directions:

1. In a bowl, mix the beef with the onion, chili powder and the other ingredients except the oil, stir well and shape your meatloaf.
2. Grease a loaf pan that fits your Crock Pot with the oil, add meatloaf mix into the pan, put it in your Crock Pot, put the lid on and cook on Low for 4 hours.
3. Slice and serve for breakfast.

Nutrition Info:

- calories 200, fat 6, fiber 12, carbs 17, protein 10

Broccoli Omelet

Servings: 4

Cooking Time: 2 Hours

Ingredients:

- 5 eggs, beaten
- 1 tablespoon cream cheese
- 3 oz broccoli, chopped
- 1 tomato, chopped
- 1 teaspoon avocado oil

Directions:

1. Mix eggs with cream cheese and transfer in the Crock Pot.
2. Add avocado oil, broccoli, and tomato.
3. Close the lid and cook the omelet on High for 2 hours.

Nutrition Info:

- Per Serving: 99 calories, 7.9g protein, 2.6g carbohydrates, 6.6g fat, 0.8g fiber, 207mg cholesterol, 92mg sodium, 184mg potassium.

Chocolate French Toast

Servings: 4

Cooking Time: 4 Hours

Ingredients:

- Cooking spray
- 1 loaf of bread, cubed
- ¾ cup brown sugar
- 3 eggs
- 1 and ½ cups milk
- 1 teaspoon vanilla extract
- ¾ cup chocolate chips
- 1 teaspoon cinnamon powder

Directions:

1. Grease your Crock Pot with the cooking spray and arrange bread cubes inside.
2. In a bowl, mix the eggs with milk, sugar, vanilla, cinnamon and chocolate chips, whisk well, add to the Crock Pot, cover and cook on Low for 4 hours.
3. Divide into bowls and serve for breakfast.

Nutrition Info:

- calories 261, fat 6, fiber 5, carbs 19, protein 6

Sweet Pepper Boats

Servings: 4

Cooking Time: 3 Hrs

Ingredients:

- 2 red sweet pepper, cut in half
- 7 oz. ground chicken
- 5 oz. Parmesan, cubed
- 1 tbsp sour cream
- 1 tbsp flour
- 1 egg
- 2 tsp almond milk
- 1 tsp salt
- ½ tsp ground black pepper
- ¼ tsp butter

Directions:

1. Take the ground chicken in a large bowl.
2. Stir in sour cream, flour, almond milk, butter, whisked eggs, and black pepper.
3. Mix well and divide this chicken mixture in the sweet peppers.
4. Top each stuffed pepper with cheese cube.
5. Put the cooker's lid on and set the cooking time to 3 hours on High settings.
6. Serve warm.

Nutrition Info:

- Per Serving: Calories 261, Total Fat 8.9g, Fiber 1g, Total Carbs 19.15g, Protein 26g

Raisins And Rice Pudding

Servings: 4

Cooking Time: 6 Hours

Ingredients:

- 1 cup long-grain rice
- 2.5 cups organic almond milk
- 2 tablespoons cornstarch
- 1 teaspoon vanilla extract
- 2 tablespoons raisins, chopped

Directions:

1. Put all ingredients in the Crock Pot and carefully mix.
2. Then close the lid and cook the pudding for 6 hours on Low.

Nutrition Info:

- Per Serving: 238 calories, 4.1g protein, 49.4g carbohydrates, 1.9g fat, 0.8g fiber, 0mg cholesterol, 91mg sodium, 89mg potassium

Meat Buns

Servings: 4

Cooking Time: 6 Hours

Ingredients:

- 1 cup ground pork
- ½ cup ground chicken
- 1 tablespoon semolina
- 1 teaspoon dried oregano
- 1 teaspoon butter, melted
- 1 teaspoon salt

Directions:

1. Mix ground pork with ground chicken.
2. Add semolina, dried oregano, and salt.
3. Then add butter and stir the meat mixture until homogenous.
4. Transfer it in the silicon bun molds.
5. Put the molds with buns in the Crock Pot.
6. Close the lid and cook them on Low for 6 hours.

Nutrition Info:

- Per Serving: 110 calories, 10.4g protein, 2.1g carbohydrates, 6.3g fat, 0.3g fiber, 37mg cholesterol, 623mg sodium, 54mg potassium

Nutty Sweet Potatoes

Servings: 8

Cooking Time: 6 Hrs

Ingredients:

- 2 tbsp peanut butter
- ¼ cup peanuts
- 1 lb. sweet potato, peeled and cut in strips.
- 1 garlic clove, peeled and sliced
- 2 tbsp lemon juice
- 1 cup onion, chopped
- ½ cup chicken stock
- 1 tsp salt
- 1 tsp paprika
- 1 tsp ground black pepper

Directions:

1. Toss the sweet potato with lemon juice, paprika, salt, black pepper, and peanut butter in a large bowl.
2. Place the sweet potatoes in the Crock Pot.
3. Add onions and garlic clove on top of the potatoes.
4. Put the cooker's lid on and set the cooking time to 6 hours on Low settings.
5. Serve with crushed peanuts on top.
6. Devour.

Nutrition Info:

- Per Serving: Calories 376, Total Fat 22.4g, Fiber 6g, Total Carbs 39.36g, Protein 5g

Cheesy Sausage Casserole

Servings: 6-8

Cooking Time: 4-5 Hours

Ingredients:

- 1 ½ cups cheddar cheese, shredded
- ½ cup mayonnaise
- 2 cups green cabbage, shredded
- 2 cups zucchini, diced
- ½ cup onion, diced
- 8 large eggs
- 1 lb. pork sausage
- 1 teaspoon sage, ground, dried
- 2 teaspoons prepared yellow mustard
- Cayenne pepper to taste
- ¼ teaspoon sea salt
- ¼ teaspoon black pepper

Directions:

1. Using cooking spray, grease the inside of the Crock-Pot. In a mixing bowl, whisk together eggs, mayonnaise, cheese, mustard, dried ground sage, cayenne pepper, salt, and black pepper. Layer half of the sausage, cabbage, zucchini, and onions into the Crock-Pot. Repeat with the remaining ingredients of zucchini, onion, sausage and cabbage. Pour the egg mixture onto the layered ingredients. Cook for 4-5 hours on LOW, until it is golden brown on the edges and set. Serve warm.

Nutrition Info:

- Calories: 484, Total Fat: 38.85 g, Saturated Fat: 21.6 g, Net Carbs: 6.39 g, Dietary Fiber: 1.8 g, Protein: 26.4 g

Raspberry Chia Pudding

Servings:2

Cooking Time: 2 Hours

Ingredients:

- 4 tablespoons chia seeds
- 1 cup of coconut milk
- 2 teaspoons raspberries

Directions:

1. Put chia seeds and coconut milk in the Crock Pot and cook it for 2 hours on Low.
2. Then transfer the cooked chia pudding in the glasses and top with raspberries.

Nutrition Info:

- Per Serving: 423 calories, 7.7g protein, 19.6g carbohydrates, 37.9g fat, 13.1g fiber, 0mg cholesterol, 23mg sodium, 442mg potassium.

Cocoa And Berries Quinoa

Servings: 2

Cooking Time: 8 Hours

Ingredients:

- Cooking spray
- 1 cup quinoa
- 2 cups almond milk
- ¼ cup heavy cream
- ¼ cup blueberries
- 2 tablespoons cocoa powder
- 1 tablespoon brown sugar

Directions:

1. Grease your Crock Pot with the cooking spray, add the quinoa, berries and the other ingredients, toss, put the lid on and cook on Low for 8 hours.
2. Divide into 2 bowls and serve for breakfast.

Nutrition Info:

- calories 200, fat 4, fiber 5, carbs 17, protein 5

Beans Salad

Servings: 2

Cooking Time: 6 Hours

Ingredients:

- 1 cup canned black beans, drained
- 1 cup canned red kidney beans, drained
- 1 cup baby spinach
- 2 spring onions, chopped
- ½ red bell pepper, chopped
- ¼ teaspoon turmeric powder
- ½ teaspoon garam masala
- ¼ cup veggie stock
- A pinch of cumin, ground
- A pinch of chili powder
- A pinch of salt and black pepper
- ½ cup salsa

Directions:

1. In your Crock Pot, mix the beans with the spinach, onions and the other ingredients, toss, put the lid on and cook on High for 6 hours.
2. Divide the mix into bowls and serve for breakfast.

Nutrition Info:

- calories 130, fat 4, fiber 2, carbs 5, protein 4

Sweet Pepper Eggs

Servings:2

Cooking Time: 2.5 Hours

Ingredients:

- 1 sweet pepper
- 4 eggs
- ¼ teaspoon ground black pepper
- 1 teaspoon butter, melted

Directions:

1. Slice the sweet pepper into 4 rounds.
2. Then brush the Crock Pot with butter from inside.
3. Put the sweet pepper rounds in the Crock Pot in one layer.
4. Then crack the eggs in the sweet pepper rounds.
5. Sprinkle the eggs with ground black pepper and close the lid.
6. Cook the meal on High for 2.5 hours.

Nutrition Info:

- Per Serving: 162 calories, 11.7g protein, 5.4g carbohydrates, 10.8g fat, 0.9g fiber, 332mg cholesterol, 138mg sodium, 234mg potassium.

Appetizers Recipes

Appetizers Recipes

Spicy Monterey Jack Fondue

Servings: 6

Cooking Time: 4 1/4 Hours

Ingredients:

- 1 garlic clove
- 1 cup white wine
- 2 cups grated Monterey Jack cheese
- 1/2 cup grated Parmesan
- 1 red chili, seeded and chopped
- 1 tablespoon cornstarch
- 1/2 cup milk
- 1 pinch nutmeg
- 1 pinch salt
- 1 pinch ground black pepper

Directions:

1. Rub the inside of your Crock Pot's pot with a garlic clove just to infuse it with aroma.
2. Add the white wine into the pot and stir in the cheeses, red chili, cornstarch and milk.
3. Season with nutmeg, salt and black pepper and cook on low heat for 4 hours.
4. The fondue is best served warm with bread sticks or vegetables.

Caramelized Onion And Cranberry Dip

Servings: 16

Cooking Time: 6 1/4 Hours

Ingredients:

- 2 tablespoons olive oil
- 4 red onions, sliced
- 1 apple, peeled and diced
- 1 cup frozen cranberries
- 1/4 cup balsamic vinegar
- 1/4 cup fresh orange juice
- 2 tablespoons brown sugar
- 1 teaspoon orange zest
- 1 bay leaf
- 1 thyme sprig
- 1 teaspoon salt

Directions:

1. Heat the oil in a skillet and stir in the onions. Cook for 10 minutes until the onions begin to caramelize.
2. Transfer the onions in a Crock Pot and stir in the remaining ingredients.
3. Cover with a lid and cook on low settings for 6 hours.
4. Serve the dip chilled.

Artichoke Dip

Servings: 20

Cooking Time: 6 1/4 Hours

Ingredients:

- 2 sweet onions, chopped
- 1 red chili, chopped
- 2 garlic cloves, chopped
- 1 jar artichoke hearts, drained and chopped
- 1 cup cream cheese
- 1 cup heavy cream
- 2 oz. blue cheese, crumbled
- 2 tablespoons chopped cilantro

Directions:

1. Mix the onions, chili, garlic, artichoke hearts, cream cheese, heavy cream and blue cheese in a Crock Pot.
2. Cook on low settings for 6 hours.
3. When done, stir in the cilantro and serve the dip warm or chilled.

Southwestern Nacho Dip

Servings: 10

Cooking Time: 6 1/4 Hours

Ingredients:

- 1 pound ground pork
- 1 cup apple juice
- 4 garlic cloves, chopped
- 2 cups BBQ sauce
- 2 tablespoons brown sugar
- Salt and pepper to taste
- 1 1/2 cups sweet corn
- 1 can black beans, drained
- 1 cup diced tomatoes
- 2 jalapeno peppers, chopped
- 2 tablespoons chopped cilantro
- 2 cups grated Cheddar
- 1 lime, juiced
- Nachos for serving

Directions:

1. Heat a skillet over medium flame and add the pork. Cook for a few minutes, stirring often.
2. Transfer the pork in your Crock Pot and add the apple juice, garlic, BBQ sauce, brown sugar, salt and pepper.
3. Cook on high settings for 2 hours.
4. After 2 hours, add the remaining ingredients and continue cooking for 4 hours on low settings.
5. Serve the dip warm with nachos.

Chili Corn Cheese Dip

Servings: 8

Cooking Time: 2 1/4 Hours

Ingredients:

- 1 pound ground beef
- 2 tablespoons olive oil
- 1 shallot, chopped
- 1 can sweet corn, drained
- 1 can kidney beans, drained
- 1/2 cup beef stock
- 1 cup diced tomatoes
- 1/2 cup black olives, pitted and chopped
- 1 teaspoon dried oregano
- 1/2 teaspoon chili powder
- 1/2 teaspoon cumin powder
- 1/4 teaspoon garlic powder
- 2 cups grated Cheddar cheese
- Tortilla chips for serving

Directions:

1. Heat the oil in a skillet and stir in the ground beef. Cook for 5-7 minutes, stirring often.
2. Transfer the meat in a Crock Pot and add the remaining ingredients.
3. Add salt and pepper to taste and cover with its lid.
4. Cook on high settings for 2 hours.
5. Serve the dip warm with tortilla chips.

Tahini Cheese Dip

Servings: 8

Cooking Time: 2 1/4 Hours

Ingredients:

- 1/2 cup tahini paste
- 1 cup whole milk
- 1/8 teaspoon garlic powder
- 1/2 teaspoon cumin powder
- 1/4 pound grated Gruyere
- 1/4 cup grated Emmentaler cheese
- Salt and pepper to taste
- 1 pinch nutmeg

Directions:

1. Combine all the ingredients in your Crock Pot.
2. Add salt and pepper if needed and cover the pot with its lid.
3. Cook on high settings for 2 hours.
4. Serve the dip warm.

Four Cheese Dip

Servings: 8

Cooking Time: 4 1/4 Hours

Ingredients:

- 1/2 pound fresh Italian sausages, skins removed
- 2 tablespoons olive oil
- 1 cup tomato sauce
- 1 cup cottage cheese
- 1 cup shredded mozzarella cheese
- 1/2 cup grated Parmesan cheese
- 1 cup grated Cheddar cheese
- 1/2 teaspoon dried thyme
- 1/2 teaspoon dried basil
- Salt and pepper to taste

Directions:

1. Heat the oil in a skillet and stir in the sausages. Cook for 5 minutes, stirring often then transfer the sausages in a Crock Pot.
2. Add the remaining ingredients and season with salt and pepper.
3. Cook on low settings for 4 hours.
4. The dip is best served warm.

Turkey Meatloaf

Servings: 8

Cooking Time: 6 1/4 Hours

Ingredients:

- 1 1/2 pounds ground turkey
- 1 carrot, grated
- 1 sweet potato, grated
- 1 egg
- 1/4 cup breadcrumbs
- 1/4 teaspoon chili powder
- Salt and pepper to taste
- 1 cup shredded mozzarella

Directions:

1. Mix all the ingredients in a bowl and season with salt and pepper as needed.
2. Give it a good mix then transfer the mixture in your Crock Pot.
3. Level the mixture well and cover with the pot's lid.
4. Cook on low settings for 6 hours.
5. Serve the meatloaf warm or chilled.

Marmalade Glazed Meatballs

Servings: 8

Cooking Time: 7 1/2 Hours

Ingredients:

- 2 pounds ground pork
- 1 shallot, chopped
- 4 garlic cloves, minced
- 1 carrot, grated
- 1 egg
- Salt and pepper to taste
- 1 cup orange marmalade
- 2 cups BBQ sauce
- 1 bay leaf
- 1 teaspoon Worcestershire sauce
- Salt and pepper to taste

Directions:

1. Mix the ground pork, shallot, garlic, carrot, egg, salt and pepper in a bowl.
2. Form small meatballs and place them on your working surface.
3. For the sauce, mix the orange marmalade, sauce, bay leaf, Worcestershire sauce, salt and pepper in your Crock Pot.
4. Place the meatballs in the sauce. Cover with its lid and cook on low settings for 7 hours.
5. Serve the meatballs warm.

Honey Glazed Chicken Drumsticks

Servings: 8

Cooking Time: 7 1/4 Hours

Ingredients:

- 3 pounds chicken drumsticks
- 1/4 cup soy sauce
- 1/4 cup honey
- 1 teaspoon rice vinegar
- 1/2 teaspoon sesame oil
- 2 tablespoons tomato paste
- 1/2 teaspoon dried Thai basil

Directions:

1. Combine all the ingredients in your Crock Pot and toss them around until the drumsticks are evenly coated.
2. Cover the pot with its lid and cook on low settings for 7 hours.
3. Serve the chicken drumsticks warm or chilled.

Cranberry Sauce Meatballs

Servings: 12

Cooking Time: 7 1/2 Hours

Ingredients:

- 3 pounds ground pork
- 1 pound ground turkey
- 1 egg
- 1/2 cup breadcrumbs
- 1 shallot, chopped
- 1/2 teaspoon ground cloves
- Salt and pepper to taste
- 2 cups cranberry sauce
- 1 cup BBQ sauce
- 1 teaspoon hot sauce
- 1 thyme sprig

Directions:

1. Mix the ground pork, turkey, egg, breadcrumbs, shal-

lot, ground cloves, salt and pepper and mix well.
2. In the meantime, combine the cranberry sauce, BBQ sauce, hot sauce and thyme sprig in your Crock Pot.
3. Form small meatballs and drop them in the sauce.
4. Cook on low settings for 7 hours.
5. Serve the meatballs warm or chilled.

Creamy Spinach Dip

Servings: 30

Cooking Time: 2 1/4 Hours

Ingredients:

- 1 can crab meat, drained
- 1 pound fresh spinach, chopped
- 2 shallots, chopped
- 2 jalapeno peppers, chopped
- 1 cup grated Parmesan
- 1/2 cup whole milk
- 1 cup sour cream
- 1 cup cream cheese
- 1 cup grated Cheddar cheese
- 1 tablespoon sherry vinegar
- 2 garlic cloves, chopped

Directions:

1. Combine all the ingredients in your Crock Pot.
2. Cover with its lid and cook on high settings for 2 hours.
3. Serve the spinach dip warm or chilled with vegetable stick or your favorite salty snacks.

Spiced Buffalo Wings

Servings: 8

Cooking Time: 8 1/4 Hours

Ingredients:

- 4 pounds chicken wings
- 1 cup BBQ sauce
- 1/4 cup butter, melted
- 1 tablespoon Worcestershire sauce
- 1 teaspoon dried oregano
- 1 teaspoon dried basil
- 1 teaspoon onion powder
- 1 teaspoon garlic powder
- 1/2 teaspoon cumin powder
- 1/2 teaspoon cinnamon powder
- 1 teaspoon hot sauce
- 1 teaspoon salt

Directions:

1. Combine all the ingredients in a Crock Pot.
2. Mix until the wings are evenly coated.
3. Cook on low settings for 8 hours.
4. Serve warm or chilled.

Blue Cheese Chicken Wings

Servings: 8

Cooking Time: 7 1/4 Hours

Ingredients:

- 4 pounds chicken wings
- 1/2 cup buffalo sauce
- 1/2 cup spicy tomato sauce
- 1 tablespoon tomato paste
- 2 tablespoons apple cider vinegar
- 1 tablespoon Worcestershire sauce
- 1 cup sour cream
- 2 oz. blue cheese, crumbled
- 1 thyme sprig

Directions:

1. Combine the buffalo sauce, tomato sauce, vinegar, Worcestershire sauce, sour cream, blue cheese and thyme in a Crock Pot.
2. Add the chicken wings and toss them until evenly coated.
3. Cook on low settings for 7 hours.
4. Serve the chicken wings preferably warm.

Asian Marinated Mushrooms

Servings: 8

Cooking Time: 8 1/4 Hours

Ingredients:

- 2 pounds mushrooms
- 1 cup soy sauce
- 1 cup water
- 1/2 cup brown sugar
- 1/4 cup rice vinegar
- 1/2 teaspoon chili powder

Directions:

1. Combine all the ingredients in your Crock Pot.
2. Cover the crock pot and cook on low settings for 8 hours.
3. Allow to cool in the pot before serving.

Cheeseburger Meatballs

Servings 8

Cooking Time 6 14 Hours

Ingredients:

- 2 pounds ground pork
- 1 shallot, chopped
- 2 tablespoons beef stock
- 1 egg
- 14 cup breadcrumbs
- 1 teaspoon Cajun seasoning
- 12 teaspoon dried basil
- Salt and pepper to taste
- 2 cups shredded processed cheese

Directions:

1. Mix the pork, shallot, beef stock, egg, breadcrumbs, Cajun seasoning and basil in a bowl.
2. Add salt and pepper to taste and mix well.
3. Form small meatballs and place them in the Crock Pot.
4. Top with shredded cheese and cook on low settings for 6 hours.
5. Serve the meatballs warm.

Pretzel Party Mix

Servings: 10

Cooking Time: 2 1/4 Hours

Ingredients:

- 4 cups pretzels
- 1 cup peanuts
- 1 cup pecans
- 1 cup crispy rice cereals
- 1/4 cup butter, melted
- 1 teaspoon Worcestershire sauce
- 1 teaspoon salt
- 1 teaspoon garlic powder

Directions:

1. Combine the pretzels, peanuts, pecans and rice cereals in your Crock Pot.
2. Drizzle with melted butter and Worcestershire sauce and mix well then sprinkle with salt and garlic powder.
3. Cover and cook on high settings for 2 hours, mixing once during cooking.
4. Allow to cool before serving.

Beer Cheese Fondue

Servings: 8

Cooking Time: 2 1/4 Hours

Ingredients:

- 1 shallot, chopped
- 1 garlic clove, minced
- 1 cup grated Gruyere cheese
- 2 cups grated Cheddar
- 1 tablespoon cornstarch
- 1 teaspoon Dijon mustard
- 1/2 teaspoon cumin seeds
- 1 cup beer
- Salt and pepper to taste

Directions:

1. Combine the shallot, garlic, cheeses, cornstarch, mustard, cumin seeds and beer in your Crock Pot.
2. Add salt and pepper to taste and mix well.
3. Cover the pot with its lid and cook on high settings for 2 hours.
4. Serve the fondue warm.

Chili Chicken Wings

Servings: 8

Cooking Time: 7 1/4 Hours

Ingredients:

- 4 pounds chicken wings
- 1/4 cup maple syrup
- 1 teaspoon garlic powder
- 1 teaspoon chili powder
- 2 tablespoons balsamic vinegar
- 1 tablespoon Dijon mustard
- 1 teaspoon Worcestershire sauce
- 1/2 cup tomato sauce
- 1 teaspoon salt

Directions:

1. Combine the chicken wings and the remaining ingredients in a Crock Pot.
2. Toss around until evenly coated and cook on low settings for 7 hours.
3. Serve the chicken wings warm or chilled.

Spicy Enchilada Dip

Servings: 8

Cooking Time: 6 1/4 Hours

Ingredients:

- 1 pound ground chicken
- 1/2 teaspoon chili powder
- 1 shallot, chopped
- 2 garlic cloves, chopped
- 1 red bell pepper, cored and diced
- 2 tomatoes, diced
- 1 cup tomato sauce
- Salt and pepper to taste
- 1 1/2 cups grated Cheddar cheese

Directions:

1. Combine the ground chicken with chili powder, shallot and garlic in your Crock Pot.
2. Add the remaining ingredients and cook on low settings for 6 hours.
3. Serve the dip warm with tortilla chips.

Vegetable & Vegetarian Recipes

Vegetable & Vegetarian Recipes

Swedish Style Beets

Servings:4

Cooking Time: 8 Hours

Ingredients:

- 1-pound beets
- ¼ cup apple cider vinegar
- 1 tablespoon olive oil
- 1 teaspoon salt
- ½ teaspoon sugar
- 3 cups of water

Directions:

1. Put beets in the Crock Pot.
2. Add water and cook the vegetables for 8 hours on Low.
3. Then drain water and peel the beets.
4. Chop the beets roughly and put in the big bowl.
5. Add all remaining ingredients and leave the beets for 2-3 hours to marinate.

Nutrition Info:

- Per Serving: 85 calories, 1.9g protein, 11.9g carbohydrates, 3.7g fat, 2.3g fiber, 0mg cholesterol, 675mg sodium, 359mg potassium.

Okra Curry

Servings:4

Cooking Time: 2.5 Hours

Ingredients:

- 1 cup potatoes, chopped
- 1 cup okra, chopped
- 1 cup tomatoes, chopped
- 1 teaspoon curry powder
- 1 teaspoon dried dill
- 1 cup coconut cream
- 1 cup of water

Directions:

1. Pour water in the Crock Pot.
2. Add coconut cream, potatoes, tomatoes, curry powder, and dried dill.
3. Cook the ingredients on High for 2 hours.
4. Then add okra and carefully mix the meal.
5. Cook it for 30 minutes on High.

Nutrition Info:

- Per Serving: 184 calories, 3g protein, 13.3g carbohydrates, 14.6g fat, 3.8g fiber, 0mg cholesterol, 18mg sodium, 508mg potassium.

Paprika Baby Carrot

Servings:2

Cooking Time: 2.5 Hours

Ingredients:

- 1 tablespoon ground paprika
- 2 cups baby carrot
- 1 teaspoon cumin seeds
- 1 cup of water
- 1 teaspoon vegan butter

Directions:

1. Pour water in the Crock Pot.
2. Add baby carrot, cumin seeds, and ground paprika.
3. Close the lid and cook the carrot on High for 2.5 hours.
4. Then drain water, add butter, and shake the vegetables.

Nutrition Info:

- Per Serving: 60 calories, 1.6g protein, 8.6g carbohydrates, 2.7g fat, 4.2g fiber, 5mg cholesterol, 64mg sodium, 220mg potassium.

Fragrant Appetizer Peppers

Servings: 2

Cooking Time: 1.5 Hours

Ingredients:

- 4 sweet peppers, seeded
- ¼ cup apple cider vinegar
- 1 red onion, sliced
- 1 teaspoon peppercorns
- ½ teaspoon sugar
- ¼ cup of water
- 1 tablespoon olive oil

Directions:

1. Slice the sweet peppers roughly and put in the Crock Pot.
2. Add all remaining ingredients and close the lid.
3. Cook the peppers on high for 1.5 hours.
4. Then cool the peppers well and store them in the fridge for up to 6 days.

Nutrition Info:

- Per Serving: 171 calories, 3.1g protein, 25.1g carbohydrates, 7.7g fat, 4.7g fiber, 0mg cholesterol, 11mg sodium, 564mg potassium.

Rice Stuffed Eggplants

Servings: 4

Cooking Time: 8 Hrs

Ingredients:

- 4 medium eggplants
- 1 cup rice, half-cooked
- ½ cup chicken stock
- 1 tsp salt
- 1 tsp paprika
- ½ cup fresh cilantro
- 3 tbsp tomato sauce
- 1 tsp olive oil

Directions:

1. Slice the eggplants in half and scoop 2/3 of the flesh from the center to make boats.
2. Mix rice with tomato sauce, paprika, salt, and cilantro in a bowl.
3. Now divide this rice mixture into the eggplant boats.
4. Pour stock and oil into the Crock Pot and place the eggplants in it.
5. Put the cooker's lid on and set the cooking time to 8 hours on Low settings.
6. Serve warm.

Nutrition Info:

- Per Serving: Calories 277, Total Fat 9.1g, Fiber 24g, Total Carbs 51.92g, Protein 11g

Quinoa Fritters

Servings: 4

Cooking Time: 1 Hour

Ingredients:

- 1 sweet potato, peeled, boiled, grated
- ½ cup quinoa, cooked
- 1 teaspoon chili powder
- 1 teaspoon salt
- 2 eggs, beaten
- 3 tablespoons cornflour
- 1 tablespoon coconut oil, melted

Directions:

1. In the mixing bowl mix grated sweet potato, quinoa, chili powder, salt, cornflour, and eggs.
2. Make the small fritters and put them in the Crock Pot.
3. Add coconut oil and close the lid.
4. Cook the fritters on High for 1 hour.

Nutrition Info:

- Per Serving: 187 calories, 6.8g protein, 24.3g carbohydrates, 7.3g fat, 3.1g fiber, 82mg cholesterol, 630mg sodium, 314mg potassium.

Parmesan Scallops Potatoes

Servings:5

Cooking Time: 7 Hours

Ingredients:

- 5 potatoes
- 5 teaspoons vegan butter
- 1 teaspoon ground black pepper
- 1 teaspoon garlic powder
- 2 tablespoons flour
- 3 cups of milk
- 3 oz vegan Parmesan, grated

Directions:

1. Peel and slice the potatoes.
2. Then place the sliced potato in the Crock Pot in one layer.
3. Sprinkle the vegetables with ground black pepper, garlic powder, and butter.
4. After this, mix flour with milk and pour over the potatoes.
5. Then sprinkle the vegetables with Parmesan and close the lid.
6. Cook the meal on Low for 7 hours.

Nutrition Info:

- Per Serving: 323 calories, 14.4g protein, 44.3g carbohydrates, 10.7g fat, 5.4g fiber, 34mg cholesterol, 267mg sodium, 967mg potassium.

Cauliflower Stuffing

Servings:4

Cooking Time: 5 Hours

Ingredients:

- 1-pound cauliflower, chopped
- ½ cup panko breadcrumbs
- 1 cup Mozzarella, shredded
- 1 cup of coconut milk
- 2 tablespoons sour cream
- 1 teaspoon onion powder

Directions:

1. Put all ingredients in the Crock Pot and carefully mix.
2. Then close the lid and cook the stuffing on low for 5 hours.
3. Cool the stuffing for 10-15 minutes and transfer in the bowls.

Nutrition Info:

- Per Serving: 236 calories, 6.9g protein, 17.8g carbohydrates, 17.2g fat, 5.2g fiber, 6mg cholesterol, 158mg sodium, 516mg potassium.

Mushroom Bourguignon

Servings:3

Cooking Time: 7 Hours

Ingredients:

- ½ cup mushrooms, chopped
- ¼ cup onion, chopped
- ¼ cup carrot, diced
- ½ cup green peas, frozen
- 1 teaspoon dried thyme
- 1 teaspoon salt
- 2 tablespoons tomato paste
- 3 cups vegetable stock

Directions:

1. Mix vegetable stock with tomato paste and pour liquid in the Crock Pot.
2. Add all remaining ingredients and close the lid.
3. Cook the meal on Low for 7 hours.

Nutrition Info:

- Per Serving: 45 calories, 2.8g protein, 8.8g carbohydrates, 0.3g fat, 2.9g fiber, 0mg cholesterol, 844mg sodium, 250mg potassium.

Zucchini Caviar

Servings: 4

Cooking Time: 5 Hours

Ingredients:

- 4 cups zucchini, grated
- 2 onions, diced
- 2 tablespoons tomato paste
- 1 teaspoon salt
- 1 teaspoon ground black pepper
- 1 cup of water
- 1 teaspoon olive oil

Directions:

1. Put all ingredients in the Crock Pot.
2. Close the lid and cook the meal on Low for 5 hours.
3. Then carefully stir the caviar and cool it to the room temperature.

Nutrition Info:

- Per Serving: 58 calories, 2.4g protein, 10.8g carbohydrates, 1.5g fat, 2.9g fiber, 0mg cholesterol, 605mg sodium, 465mg potassium.

Cauliflower Hash

Servings: 4

Cooking Time: 2.5 Hours

Ingredients:

- 3 cups cauliflower, roughly chopped
- ½ cup potato, chopped
- 3 oz Provolone, grated
- 2 tablespoons chives, chopped
- 1 cup milk
- ½ cup of water
- 1 teaspoon chili powder

Directions:

1. Pour water and milk in the Crock Pot.
2. Add cauliflower, potato, chives, and chili powder.
3. Close the lid and cook the mixture on high for 2 hours.
4. Then sprinkle the hash with provolone cheese and cook the meal on High for 30 minutes.

Nutrition Info:

- Per Serving: 134 calories, 9.3g protein, 9.5g carbohydrates, 7.1g fat, 2.4g fiber, 20mg cholesterol, 246mg sodium, 348mg potassium

Pinto Beans With Rice

Servings: 6

Cooking Time: 3 Hrs

Ingredients:

- 1 lb. pinto beans, dried
- 1/3 cup hot sauce
- Salt and black pepper to the taste
- 1 tbsp garlic, minced
- 1 tsp garlic powder
- ½ tsp cumin, ground
- 1 tbsp chili powder
- 3 bay leaves
- ½ tsp oregano, dried
- 1 cup white rice, cooked

Directions:

1. Add pinto beans along with the rest of the ingredients to your Crock Pot.
2. Put the cooker's lid on and set the cooking time to 3 hours on High settings.
3. Serve warm on top of rice.

Nutrition Info:

- Per Serving: Calories 381, Total Fat 7g, Fiber 12g, Total Carbs 35g, Protein 10g

Pumpkin Hummus

Servings:6

Cooking Time: 4 Hours

Ingredients:

- 1 cup chickpeas, canned
- 1 tablespoon tahini paste
- 1 cup pumpkin, chopped
- 1 teaspoon harissa
- 2 cups of water
- 2 tablespoons olive oil
- 1 tablespoon lemon juice

Directions:

1. Pour water in the Crock Pot.
2. Add pumpkin and cook it for 4 hours on High or until the pumpkin is soft.
3. After this, drain water and transfer the pumpkin in the food processor.
4. Add all remaining ingredients and blend the mixture until smooth.
5. Add water from pumpkin if the cooked hummus is very thick.

Nutrition Info:

- Per Serving: 193 calories, 7.4g protein, 24.4g carbohydrates, 8.3g fat, 7.2g fiber, 0mg cholesterol, 26mg sodium, 390mg potassium.

Green Peas Risotto

Servings: 6

Cooking Time: 3 Hrs 30 Minutes

Ingredients:

- 7 oz. Parmigiano-Reggiano
- 2 cup chicken broth
- 1 tsp olive oil
- 1 onion, chopped
- ½ cup green peas
- 1 garlic clove, peeled and sliced
- 2 cups long-grain rice
- ¼ cup dry wine
- 1 tsp salt
- 1 tsp ground black pepper
- 1 carrot, chopped
- 1 cup beef broth

Directions:

1. Layer a nonstick skillet with olive oil and place it over medium heat.
2. Stir in carrot and onion, then sauté for 3 minutes.
3. Transfer these veggies to the Crock Pot.
4. Add rice to the remaining oil to the skillet.
5. Stir cook for 1 minute then transfers the rice to the cooker.
6. Add garlic, dry wine, green peas, black pepper, beef broth, and chicken broth.
7. Put the cooker's lid on and set the cooking time to 3 hours on Low settings.
8. Add Parmigiano-Reggiano to the risotto.
9. Put the cooker's lid on and set the cooking time to 30 minutes on Low settings.
10. Serve warm.

Nutrition Info:

- Per Serving: Calories 268, Total Fat 3g, Fiber 4g, Total Carbs 53.34g, Protein 7g

Beans Bake

Servings:4

Cooking Time: 5 Hours

Ingredients:

- 1-pound green beans
- 1 tablespoon olive oil
- 1 teaspoon salt
- ½ teaspoon ground black pepper
- 2 tablespoons breadcrumbs
- 4 eggs, beaten

Directions:

1. Chop the green beans roughly and sprinkle them with salt and ground black pepper.
2. Then put them in the Crock Pot.
3. Sprinkle the vegetables with breadcrumbs and eggs.
4. Close the lid and cook the beans bake on Low for 5 hours.

Nutrition Info:

- Per Serving: 142 calories, 8.1g protein, 11g carbohydrates, 8.2g fat, 4.1g fiber, 164mg cholesterol, 675mg sodium, 306mg potassium.

Vegan Pepper Bowl

Servings:4

Cooking Time: 3.5 Hours

Ingredients:

- 2 cups bell pepper, sliced
- 1 tablespoon olive oil
- 1 tablespoon apple cider vinegar
- 4 tablespoons water
- 5 oz tofu, chopped
- ½ cup of coconut milk
- 1 teaspoon curry powder

Directions:

1. Put the sliced bell peppers in the Crock Pot.
2. Sprinkle them with olive oil, apple cider vinegar, and water.
3. Close the lid and cook the vegetables on low for 3 hours.
4. Meanwhile, mix curry powder with coconut milk. Put the tofu in the curry mixture and leave for 15 minutes.
5. Add the tofu and all remaining curry mixture in the Crock Pot. Gently mix it and cook for 30 minutes on low.

Nutrition Info:

- Per Serving: 145 calories, 4.3g protein, 7.1g carbohydrates, 12.4g fat, 2g fiber, 0mg cholesterol, 11mg sodium, 254mg potassium.

Sweet Potato Puree

Servings:2

Cooking Time: 4 Hours

Ingredients:

- 2 cups sweet potato, chopped
- 1 cup of water
- ¼ cup half and half
- 1 oz scallions, chopped
- 1 teaspoon salt

Directions:

1. Put sweet potatoes in the Crock Pot.
2. Add water and salt.
3. Cook them on High for 4 hours.
4. The drain water and transfer the sweet potatoes in the food processor.
5. Add half and half and blend until smooth.
6. Transfer the puree in the bowl, and scallions, and mix carefully.

Nutrition Info:

- Per Serving: 225 calories, 5.2g protein, 43.7g carbohydrates, 3.9g fat, 7g fiber, 11mg cholesterol, 1253mg sodium, 1030mg potassium.

Sautéed Greens

Servings: 4

Cooking Time: 1 Hour

Ingredients:

- 1 cup spinach, chopped
- 2 cups collard greens, chopped
- 1 cup Swiss chard, chopped
- 2 cups of water
- ½ cup half and half

Directions:

1. Put spinach, collard greens, and Swiss chard in the Crock Pot.
2. Add water and close the lid.
3. Cook the greens on High for 1 hour.
4. Then drain water and transfer the greens in the bowl.
5. Bring the half and half to boil and pour over greens.
6. Carefully mix the greens.

Nutrition Info:

- Per Serving: 49 calories, 1.8g protein, 3.2g carbohydrates, 3.7g fat, 1.1g fiber, 11mg cholesterol, 45mg sodium, 117mg potassium.

Zucchini Basil Soup

Servings: 8

Cooking Time: 3 Hours

Ingredients:

- 9 cups zucchini, diced
- 2 cups white onions, chopped
- 4 cups vegetable broth
- 8 cloves of garlic, minced
- 1 cup basil leaves
- 4 tablespoons olive oil
- Salt and pepper to taste

Directions:

1. Place the ingredients in the CrockPot.
2. Give a good stir.
3. Close the lid and cook on high for 2 hours or on low for 3 hours.
4. Once cooked, transfer into a blender and pulse until smooth.

Nutrition Info:

- Calories per serving: 93; Carbohydrates: 5.4g; Protein: 1.3g; Fat: 11.6g; Sugar: 0g; Sodium: 322mg; Fiber: 4.2g

Creamy Corn Chili

Servings: 6

Cooking Time: 6 Hrs

Ingredients:

- 2 jalapeno chilies, chopped
- 1 cup yellow onion, chopped
- 1 tbsp olive oil
- 4 poblano chilies, chopped
- 4 Anaheim chilies, chopped
- 3 cups corn
- 6 cups veggie stock
- ½ bunch cilantro, chopped
- Salt and black pepper to the taste

Directions:

1. Add jalapenos, oil, onion, poblano, corn, stock, and Anaheim chilies to the Crock Pot.
2. Put the cooker's lid on and set the cooking time to 6 hours on Low settings.
3. Puree the cooked mixture with the help of an immersion blender.
4. Stir in black pepper, salt and cilantro.
5. Serve warm.

Nutrition Info:

- Per Serving: Calories 209, Total Fat 5g, Fiber 5g, Total Carbs 33g, Protein 5g

Side Dish Recipes

Slow Cooker
Cookbook

Side Dish Recipes

Asian Sesame Asparagus

Servings: 4

Cooking Time: 4 Hrs.

Ingredients:

- 1 tbsp sesame seeds
- 1 tsp miso paste
- ¼ cup of soy sauce
- 1 cup fish stock
- 8 oz. asparagus
- 1 tsp salt
- 1 tsp chili flakes
- 1 tsp oregano
- 1 cup of water

Directions:

1. Fill the insert of the Crock Pot with water and add asparagus.
2. Put the cooker's lid on and set the cooking time to 3 hours on High settings.
3. During this time, mix miso paste with soy sauce, fish stock, and sesame seeds in a suitable bowl.
4. Stir in oregano, chili flakes, and salt, then mix well.
5. Drain the slow-cooked asparagus then return it to the Crock Pot.
6. Pour the miso-stock mixture over the asparagus.
7. Put the cooker's lid on and set the cooking time to 1 hour on High settings.
8. Serve warm.

Nutrition Info:

- Per Serving: Calories: 85, Total Fat: 4.8g, Fiber: 2g, Total Carbs: 7.28g, Protein: 4g

Veggies Rice Pilaf

Servings: 4

Cooking Time: 5 Hours

Ingredients:

- 2 cups basmati rice
- 1 cup mixed carrots, peas, corn, and green beans
- 2 cups of water
- ½ tsp green chili, minced
- ½ tsp ginger, grated
- 3 garlic cloves, minced
- 2 tbsp butter
- 1 cinnamon stick
- 1 tbsp cumin seeds
- 2 bay leaves
- 3 whole cloves
- 5 black peppercorns
- 2 whole cardamoms
- 1 tbsp sugar
- Salt to the taste

Directions:

1. Add water, rice, veggies and all other ingredients to the Crock Pot.
2. Put the cooker's lid on and set the cooking time to 5 hours on Low settings.
3. Discard the cinnamon and serve warm.

Nutrition Info:

- Per Serving: Calories: 300, Total Fat: 4g, Fiber: 3g, Total Carbs: 40g, Protein: 13g

Red Curry Veggie Mix

Servings: 2

Cooking Time: 3 Hours

Ingredients:

- 2 zucchinis, cubed
- 1 eggplant, cubed
- ½ cup button mushrooms, quartered
- 1 small red sweet potatoes, chopped
- ½ cup veggie stock
- 1 garlic cloves, minced
- ¼ tablespoon Thai red curry paste
- ¼ tablespoon ginger, grated
- Salt and black pepper to the taste
- 2 tablespoons coconut milk

Directions:

1. In your Crock Pot, mix the zucchinis with the eggplant and the other ingredients, toss, put the lid on and cook on Low for 3 hours.
2. Divide between plates and serve as a side dish.

Nutrition Info:

- calories 169, fat 2, fiber 2, carbs 15, protein 6

Cauliflower Mash

Servings: 2

Cooking Time: 5 Hours

Ingredients:

- 1 pound cauliflower florets
- ½ cup heavy cream
- 1 tablespoon dill, chopped
- 2 garlic cloves, minced
- 1 tablespoons butter, melted
- A pinch of salt and black pepper

Directions:

1. In your Crock Pot, mix the cauliflower with the cream and the other ingredients, toss, put the lid on and cook on High for 5 hours.
2. Mash the mix, whisk, divide between plates and serve.

Nutrition Info:

- calories 187, fat 4, fiber 5, carbs 7, protein 3

Zucchini Onion Pate

Servings: 6

Cooking Time: 6 Hours

Ingredients:

- 3 medium zucchinis, peeled and chopped
- 2 red onions, grated
- 6 tbsp tomato paste
- ½ cup fresh dill
- 1 tsp salt
- 1 tsp butter
- 1 tbsp brown sugar
- ½ tsp ground black pepper
- 1 tsp paprika
- ¼ chili pepper

Directions:

1. Add zucchini to the food processor and blend for 3 minutes until smooth.
2. Transfer the zucchini blend to the Crock Pot.
3. Stir in onions and all other ingredients.
4. Put the cooker's lid on and set the cooking time to 6 hours on Low settings.
5. Serve warm.

Nutrition Info:

- Per Serving: Calories: 45, Total Fat: 0.8g, Fiber: 2g, Total Carbs: 9.04g, Protein: 1g

Summer Squash Mix

Servings: 4

Cooking Time: 2 Hours

Ingredients:

- ¼ cup olive oil
- 2 tablespoons basil, chopped
- 2 tablespoons balsamic vinegar
- 2 garlic cloves, minced
- 2 teaspoons mustard
- Salt and black pepper to the taste
- 3 summer squash, sliced
- 2 zucchinis, sliced

Directions:

1. In your Crock Pot, mix squash with zucchinis, salt, pepper, mustard, garlic, vinegar, basil and oil, toss a bit, cover and cook on High for 2 hours.
2. Divide between plates and serve as a side dish.

Nutrition Info:

- calories 179, fat 13, fiber 2, carbs 10, protein 4

Turmeric Buckwheat

Servings: 6

Cooking Time: 4 Hrs

Ingredients:

- 4 tbsp milk powder
- 2 tbsp butter
- 1 carrot
- 4 cup buckwheat
- 4 cups chicken stock
- 1 tbsp salt
- 1 tbsp turmeric
- 1 tsp paprika

Directions:

1. Whisk milk powder with buckwheat, stock, salt, turmeric, and paprika in the Crock Pot.
2. Stir in carrot strips and mix gently.
3. Put the cooker's lid on and set the cooking time to 4 hours on High settings.
4. Stir in butter then serve warm.

Nutrition Info:

- Per Serving: Calories: 238, Total Fat: 6.6g, Fiber: 4g, Total Carbs: 37.85g, Protein: 9g

Buttery Artichokes

Servings: 5

Cooking Time: 6 Hrs.

Ingredients:

- 13 oz. artichoke heart halved
- 1 tsp salt
- 4 cups chicken stock
- 1 tsp turmeric
- 1 garlic clove, peeled
- 4 tbsp butter
- 4 oz. Parmesan, shredded

Directions:

1. Add artichoke, stock, salt, and turmeric to the Crock Pot.
2. Put the cooker's lid on and set the cooking time to 6 hours on Low settings.
3. Drain and transfer the cooked artichoke to the serving plates.
4. Drizzle, cheese, and butter over the artichoke.
5. Serve warm.

Nutrition Info:

- Per Serving: Calories: 272, Total Fat: 12.8g, Fiber: 4g, Total Carbs: 24.21g, Protein: 17g

Rosemary Leeks

Servings: 2

Cooking Time: 3 Hours

Ingredients:

- ½ tablespoon olive oil
- ½ leeks, sliced
- ½ cup tomato sauce
- 2 garlic cloves, minced
- Salt and black pepper to the taste
- ¼ tablespoon rosemary, chopped

Directions:

1. In your Crock Pot, mix the leeks with the oil, sauce and the other ingredients, toss, put the lid on, cook on High for 3 hours, divide between plates and serve as a side dish.

Nutrition Info:

- calories 202, fat 2, fiber 6, carbs 18, protein 8

Cheddar Potatoes Mix

Servings: 2

Cooking Time: 3 Hours

Ingredients:

- ½ pound gold potatoes, peeled and cut into wedges
- 2 ounces heavy cream
- ½ teaspoon turmeric powder
- ½ teaspoon rosemary, dried
- ¼ cup cheddar cheese, shredded
- 1 tablespoon butter, melted
- Cooking spray
- A pinch of salt and black pepper

Directions:

1. Grease your Crock Pot with the cooking spray, add the

potatoes, cream, turmeric and the other ingredients, toss, put the lid on and cook on High for 3 hours.

2. Divide between plates and serve as a side dish.

Nutrition Info:

- calories 300, fat 14, fiber 6, carbs 22, protein 6

Carrot Beet Salad

Servings: 6

Cooking Time: 7 Hours

Ingredients:

- ½ cup walnuts, chopped
- ¼ cup lemon juice
- ½ cup olive oil
- 1 shallot, chopped
- 1 tsp Dijon mustard
- 1 tbsp brown sugar
- Salt and black pepper to the taste
- 2 beets, peeled and cut into wedges
- 2 carrots, peeled and sliced
- 1 cup parsley
- 5 oz. arugula

Directions:

1. Add beets, carrots, and rest of the ingredients to the Crock Pot.
2. Put the cooker's lid on and set the cooking time to 7 hours on Low settings.
3. Serve warm.

Nutrition Info:

- Per Serving: Calories: 100, Total Fat: 3g, Fiber: 3g, Total Carbs: 7g, Protein: 3g

Zucchini Casserole

Servings: 10

Cooking Time: 2 Hours

Ingredients:

- 7 cups zucchini, sliced
- 2 cups crackers, crushed
- 2 tablespoons melted butter
- 1/3 cup yellow onion, chopped
- 1 cup cheddar cheese, shredded
- 1 cup chicken stock
- 1/3 cup sour cream
- Salt and black pepper to the taste
- 1 tablespoon parsley, chopped
- Cooking spray

Directions:

1. Grease your Crock Pot with cooking spray and arrange zucchini and onion in the pot.
2. Add melted butter, stock, sour cream, salt and pepper and toss.
3. Add cheese mixed with crackers, cover and cook on High for 2 hours.
4. Divide zucchini casserole on plates, sprinkle parsley all over and serve as a side dish.

Nutrition Info:

- calories 180, fat 6, fiber 1, carbs 14, protein 4

Classic Veggies Mix

Servings: 4

Cooking Time: 3 Hours

Ingredients:

- 1 and ½ cups red onion, cut into medium chunks
- 1 cup cherry tomatoes, halved
- 2 and ½ cups zucchini, sliced
- 2 cups yellow bell pepper, chopped
- 1 cup mushrooms, sliced
- 2 tablespoons basil, chopped
- 1 tablespoon thyme, chopped
- ½ cup olive oil
- ½ cup balsamic vinegar

Directions:

1. In your Crock Pot, mix onion pieces with tomatoes, zucchini, bell pepper, mushrooms, basil, thyme, oil and vinegar, toss to coat everything, cover and cook on High for 3 hours.
2. Divide between plates and serve as a side dish.

Nutrition Info:

- calories 150, fat 2, fiber 2, carbs 6, protein 5

Black Beans Mix(1)

Servings: 2

Cooking Time: 6 Hours

Ingredients:

- ½ pound black beans, soaked overnight and drained
- A pinch of salt and black pepper
- ½ cup veggie stock
- ½ tablespoon lime juice
- 2 tablespoons cilantro, chopped
- 2 tablespoons pine nuts

Directions:

1. In your Crock Pot, mix the beans with the stock and the other ingredients, toss, put the lid on and cook on Low for 6 hours.
2. Divide everything between plates and serve.

Nutrition Info:

- calories 200, fat 3, fiber 4, carbs 7, protein 5

Rice And Beans

Servings: 6

Cooking Time: 5 Hours

Ingredients:

- 1 pound red kidney beans, soaked overnight and drained
- Salt to the taste
- 1 teaspoon olive oil
- 1 pound smoked sausage, roughly chopped
- 1 yellow onion, chopped
- 1 celery stalk, chopped
- 4 garlic cloves, chopped
- 1 green bell pepper, chopped
- 1 teaspoon thyme, dried
- 2 bay leaves
- 5 cups water
- Long grain rice, already cooked
- 2 green onions, minced
- 2 tablespoons parsley, minced
- Hot sauce for serving

Directions:

1. In your Crock Pot, mix red beans with salt, oil, sausage, onion, celery, garlic, bell pepper, thyme, bay leaves and water, cover and cook on Low for 5 hours.
2. Divide the rice between plates, add beans, sausage and veggies on top, sprinkle green onions and parsley and serve as a side dish with hot sauce drizzled all over.

Nutrition Info:

- calories 200, fat 5, fiber 6, carbs 20, protein 5

Garlic Risotto

Servings: 2

Cooking Time: 2 Hours

Ingredients:

- 1 small shallot, chopped

- 1 cup wild rice
- 1 cup chicken stock
- 1 tablespoons olive oil
- 2 garlic cloves, minced
- Salt and black pepper to the taste
- 2 tablespoons cilantro, chopped

Directions:

1. In your Crock Pot, mix the rice with the stock, shallot and the other ingredients, toss, put the lid on and cook on High for 2 hours
2. Divide between plates and serve as a side dish.

Nutrition Info:

- calories 204, fat 7, fiber 3, carbs 17, protein 7

Hasselback Potatoes

Servings: 7

Cooking Time: 8 Hours

Ingredients:

- 7 potatoes
- 2 oz. butter
- 1 tbsp olive oil
- 1 tbsp dried dill
- 1 tsp salt
- 1 tsp paprika

Directions:

1. Use a knife to make 4 slits on top of each potato.
2. Mix butter, dill, olive oil, paprika, and salt in a bowl.
3. Layer the insert of the Crock Pot with a foil sheet.
4. Place the potatoes inside and pour the butter-dill mixture on top of them.
5. Put the cooker's lid on and set the cooking time to 8 hours on Low settings.
6. Serve warm.

Nutrition Info:

- Per Serving: Calories: 363, Total Fat: 9g, Fiber:8g, Total Carbs: 65.17g, Protein: 8g

Tomato And Corn Mix

Servings: 2

Cooking Time: 4 Hours

Ingredients:

- 1 red onion, sliced
- 2 spring onions, chopped
- 1 cup corn
- 1 cup tomatoes, cubed
- 1 tablespoon olive oil
- ½ red bell pepper, chopped
- ½ cup tomato sauce
- ¼ teaspoon sweet paprika
- ½ teaspoon cumin, ground
- 1 tablespoon chives, chopped
- Salt and black pepper to the taste

Directions:

1. Heat up a pan with the oil over medium-high heat, add the onion , spring onions and bell pepper and cook for 10 minutes.
2. Transfer the mix to the Crock Pot, add the corn and the other ingredients, toss, put the lid on and cook on Low for 4 hours.
3. Divide the mix between plates and serve as a side dish.

Nutrition Info:

- calories 312, fat 4, fiber 6, carbs 12, protein 6

Spinach Mix

Servings: 2

Cooking Time: 1 Hour

Ingredients:

- 1 pound baby spinach
- ½ cup cherry tomatoes, halved
- ½ tablespoon olive oil
- ½ cup veggie stock
- 1 small yellow onion, chopped

- ¼ teaspoon coriander, ground
- ¼ teaspoon cumin, ground
- ¼ teaspoon garam masala
- ¼ teaspoon chili powder
- Salt and black pepper to the taste

Directions:

1. In your Crock Pot, mix the spinach with the tomatoes, oil and the other ingredients, toss, put the lid on and cook on High for 1 hour.
2. Divide between plates and serve as a side dish.,

Nutrition Info:

- calories 270, fat 4, fiber 6, carbs 8, protein 12

Beans And Red Peppers

Servings: 2

Cooking Time: 2 Hrs.

Ingredients:

- 2 cups green beans, halved
- 1 red bell pepper, cut into strips
- Salt and black pepper to the taste
- 1 tbsp olive oil
- 1 and ½ tbsp honey mustard

Directions:

1. Add green beans, honey mustard, red bell pepper, oil, salt, and black to Crock Pot.
2. Put the cooker's lid on and set the cooking time to 2 hours on High settings.
3. Serve warm.

Nutrition Info:

- Per Serving: Calories: 50, Total Fat: 0g, Fiber: 4g, Total Carbs: 8g, Protein: 2g

Lunch & Dinner Recipes

Lunch & Dinner Recipes

Beans And Rice

Servings: 6

Cooking Time: 3 Hours

Ingredients:

- 1 pound pinto beans, dried
- 1/3 cup hot sauce
- Salt and black pepper to the taste
- 1 tablespoon garlic, minced
- 1 teaspoon garlic powder
- ½ teaspoon cumin, ground
- 1 tablespoon chili powder
- 3 bay leaves
- ½ teaspoon oregano, dried
- 1 cup white rice, cooked

Directions:

1. In your Crock Pot, mix pinto beans with hot sauce, salt, pepper, garlic, garlic powder, cumin, chili powder, bay leaves and oregano, stir, cover and cook on High for 3 hours.
2. Divide rice between plates, add pinto beans on top and serve for lunch

Nutrition Info:

- calories 381, fat 7, fiber 12, carbs 35, protein 10

Cheesy Three Bean Chili

Servings: 8

Cooking Time: 8 1/2 Hours

Ingredients:

- 2 tablespoons olive oil
- 2 sweet onions, chopped
- 4 garlic cloves, chopped
- 1 celery stalk, sliced
- 1 carrot, diced
- 1 cup dried black beans
- 1 cup kidney beans
- 1/2 cup red beans
- 1 can fire roasted tomatoes
- 2 bay leaves
- 2 cups vegetable stock
- 2 cups water
- Salt and pepper to taste
- 1 cup grated Cheddar for serving

Directions:

1. Heat the oil in a skillet and stir in the onions, garlic, celery and carrot. Cook on low settings for 5 minutes until softened then transfer in your crock pot.
2. Add the remaining ingredients and season with salt and pepper.
3. Cook on low settings for 8 hours and serve the chili warm, topped with grated Cheddar.

Apricot Glazed Gammon

Servings: 6-8

Cooking Time: 6 1/4 Hours

Ingredients:

- 3-4 pounds piece of gammon joint
- 1/2 cup apricot preserve
- 1 teaspoon cumin powder
- 1/4 teaspoon chili powder
- 1 cup vegetable stock
- Salt and pepper to taste

Directions:

1. Mix the apricot preserve with cumin powder and chili powder then spread this mixture over the gammon.
2. Place the meat in your Crock Pot and add the stock.
3. Cook on low settings for 6 hours.
4. Serve the gammon with your favorite side dish, warm or chilled.

Stuffed Butternut Squash

Servings: 6

Cooking Time: 6 1/2 Hours

Ingredients:

- 1 large butternut squash, halved
- 2 cups cooked lentils
- 1 shallot, chopped
- 2 garlic cloves, minced
- 1/2 teaspoon cumin powder
- 1/4 teaspoon chili powder
- Salt and pepper to taste
- 1/2 cup vegetable stock

Directions:

1. Place the butternut squash in your crock pot.
2. Mix the lentils, shallot, garlic, cumin powder and chili powder in a bowl. Add salt and pepper to taste then spoon the mixture into the butternut squash halves.
3. Add the stock in the crock pot as well and cook on low settings for 6 hours.
4. Serve the butternut squash warm and fresh.

Wild Mushroom Barley Risotto

Servings: 6

Cooking Time: 6 1/4 Hours

Ingredients:

- 2 tablespoons olive oil
- 1 shallot, chopped
- 1 celery stalk, diced
- 1 garlic clove, minced
- 1 carrot, diced
- 1 cup pearl barley
- 2 cups vegetable stock
- 1/4 cup grated Parmesan
- Salt and pepper to taste
- 1 thyme sprig

Directions:

1. Heat the oil in a skillet and add the shallot, celery, garlic and carrot. Cook for 2 minutes until softened. Transfer in your Crock Pot.
2. Add the remaining ingredients, except the Parmesan, and season with salt and pepper.
3. Cook on low settings for 6 hours.
4. When done, add the cheese and mix well.
5. Serve the risotto warm.

Parmesan Biscuit Pot Pie

Servings: 8

Cooking Time: 7 1/2 Hours

Ingredients:

- 2 tablespoons olive oil
- 2 garlic cloves, chopped
- 1 large onion, finely chopped
- 2 carrots, diced
- 1 parsnip, diced
- 1 turnip, diced
- 2 cups sliced mushrooms
- 1 cup green peas
- Salt and pepper to taste
- 1/2 cup all-purpose flour
- 1/2 teaspoon baking powder
- 1 cup grated Parmesan
- 1/4 cup butter, chilled and cubed
- 1/2 cup buttermilk

Directions:

1. Combine the oil, garlic, onion, carrots, parsnip, turnip, mushrooms, green peas, salt and pepper in your Crock Pot.
2. Combine the flour, baking powder and Parmesan in your crock pot. Mix until sandy then stir in the buttermilk.
3. Spoon the batter over the vegetables and cook on low settings for 7 hours.
4. Serve the pot pie warm or chilled.

Button Mushroom Beef Stew

Servings: 6

Cooking Time: 6 1/2 Hours

Ingredients:

- 2 pounds beef roast, cubed
- 1 tablespoon all-purpose flour
- 2 tablespoons canola oil
- 2 carrots, diced
- 1 celery root, peeled and diced
- 1 can fire roasted tomatoes
- 1 pound button mushrooms
- 1 cup beef stock
- 2 bay leaves
- 1 red chili, chopped
- Salt and pepper to taste

Directions:

1. Season the beef with salt and pepper and sprinkle it with flour.
2. Heat the oil in a frying pan and add the beef. Cook for a few minutes until golden then transfer in your Crock Pot.
3. Add the rest of the ingredients and adjust the taste with salt and pepper.
4. Cover and cook on low settings for 6 hours.
5. Serve the stew warm or chilled.

Fennel Soup

Servings: 2

Cooking Time: 4 Hours

Ingredients:

- 2 fennel bulbs, sliced
- ½ cup tomatoes, crushed
- 1 red onion, sliced
- 1 leek, chopped
- 2 cups veggie stock
- ½ teaspoon cumin, ground
- 1 tablespoon dill, chopped
- ½ tablespoon olive oil
- Salt and black pepper to the taste

Directions:

1. In your Crock Pot, mix the fennel with the tomatoes, onion and the other ingredients, toss, put the lid on and cook on High for 4 hours.
2. Ladle into bowls and serve hot.

Nutrition Info:

- calories 132, fat 2, fiber 5, carbs 11, protein 3

Veggie Chickpea Curry

Servings: 6

Cooking Time: 6 1/4 Hours

Ingredients:

- 1 cup dried chickpeas, rinsed
- 1 large onion, chopped
- 1 carrot, sliced
- 1 teaspoon curry
- 1 teaspoon grated ginger
- 2 garlic cloves, chopped
- 2 potatoes, peeled and diced
- 1 red bell pepper, cored and diced
- 1 poblano pepper, chopped
- 1 cup fire roasted tomatoes
- 2 cups vegetable stock
- Salt and pepper to taste
- 1 bay leaf
- Chopped cilantro for serving

Directions:

1. Combine all the ingredients in your Crock Pot.
2. Add salt and pepper to taste and cook the curry on low settings for 6 hours.
3. The curry is best served warm, topped with chopped cilantro.

White Bean Chili Over Creamy Grits

Servings: 8

Cooking Time: 6 3/4 Hours

Ingredients:

- 2 cups dried white beans, rinsed
- 2 cups vegetable stock
- 2 cups water
- 1 onion, chopped
- 2 garlic cloves, chopped
- 1 carrot, diced
- 1 celery stalk, diced
- 1 red chili, chopped
- 1/2 teaspoon cumin powder
- 1 cup fire roasted tomatoes
- 1 bay leaf
- 2 cups spinach, shredded
- Salt and pepper to taste
- 1 cup grits
- 2 cups whole milk
- 1 cup grated Cheddar

Directions:

1. Combine the beans, stock, water, onion, garlic, carrot, celery, red chili, tomatoes, cumin powder and bay leaf in your Crock Pot. Top with shredded spinach.
2. Add salt and pepper to taste and cook on low settings for 6 1/2 hours.
3. To make the creamy grits, pour the milk in a saucepan. Bring to a boil and add the grits. Cook on low heat until creamy then remove from heat and add the cheese.
4. Spoon the grits into the serving bowls and top with white bean stew.

Pesto Freekeh

Servings:4

Cooking Time: 2 Hours

Ingredients:

- 2 tablespoons pesto sauce
- 1 tablespoon sesame oil
- 1 oz raisins
- 1 cup freekeh
- 3 cups chicken stock

Directions:

1. Pour the chicken stock in the Crock Pot.
2. Add freekeh and raisins and cook the ingredients on High for 2 hours. The cooked freekeh should be tender.
3. Then transfer the freekeh mixture in the bowl.
4. Add sesame oil and pesto sauce.
5. Carefully mix the meal.

Nutrition Info:

- Per Serving: 125 calories, 3.5g protein, 13.2g carbohydrates, 7.4g fat, 1.4g fiber, 2mg cholesterol, 621mg sodium, 64mg potassium.

Sesame Glazed Chicken

Servings: 6

Cooking Time: 3 1/4 Hours

Ingredients:

- 6 chicken thighs
- 1 tablespoon sesame oil
- 2 tablespoon soy sauce
- 1 tablespoon brown sugar
- 2 tablespoons fresh orange juice
- 2 tablespoons hoisin sauce
- 1 teaspoon grated ginger
- 1 tablespoon cornstarch
- 2 tablespoons water
- 1 tablespoon sesame seeds

Directions:

1. Combine all the ingredients in your crock pot.
2. Cook the chicken on high settings for 3 hours.
3. Serve the chicken warm with your favorite side dish.

Root Vegetable Risotto

Servings: 6

Cooking Time: 6 1/4 Hours

Ingredients:

- 1 cup white rice
- 2 tablespoons olive oil
- 1 parsnip, diced
- 1 carrot, diced
- 1 parsley root, diced
- 1 sweet potato, peeled and diced
- 1/2 teaspoon dried sage
- Salt and pepper to taste
- 1/4 cup white wine
- 1 3/4 cups vegetable stock
- 2 tablespoons grated Parmesan

Directions:

1. Combine the rice, oil, parsnip, carrot, parsley root, potato, sage, white wine and stock in your Crock Pot.
2. Season with salt and pepper as needed and cook on low settings for 6 hours.
3. When done, stir in the grated cheese and serve the risotto warm and fresh.

Lime Bean Stew

Servings: 8

Cooking Time: 6 1/4 Hours

Ingredients:

- 2 cups dried lime beans
- 2 carrots, sliced
- 2 celery stalks, sliced
- 1 head cauliflower, cut into florets
- 1 teaspoon grated ginger
- 1 cup diced tomatoes
- 1 cup tomato sauce
- 2 cups vegetable stock
- 1 bay leaf
- 1 thyme sprig
- Salt and pepper to taste

Directions:

1. Combine the beans, carrots, celery, cauliflower, ginger, tomatoes, tomato sauce, stock, salt and pepper, as well as bay leaf and thyme in your crock pot.
2. Season with salt and pepper as needed and cook on low settings for 6 hours.
3. The stew is best served warm.

Mediterranean Beef Stew

Servings: 8

Cooking Time: 7 1/4 Hours

Ingredients:

- 2 pounds beef sirloin, cubed
- 2 tablespoons canola oil
- 1 large sweet onion, finely chopped
- 4 garlic cloves, minced
- 2 ripe tomatoes, peeled and diced
- 2 zucchinis, cubed
- 4 red bell peppers, cored and diced
- 1 cup tomato sauce
- 2 tablespoons tomato paste
- 1/2 cup fresh orange juice
- 1 teaspoon dried oregano
- 1/2 teaspoon dried basil
- Salt and pepper to taste
- 1 bay leaf
- 1 thyme sprig
- 1 rosemary sprig

Directions:

1. Heat the oil in a frying pan and add the beef sirloin. Cook for a few minutes until golden then transfer in your Crock Pot.
2. Add the remaining ingredients in the recipe and season with salt and pepper.
3. Cover the pot with a lid and cook on low settings for 8 hours.
4. Serve the stew warm or chilled.

Pork Chili

Servings: 2

Cooking Time: 10 Hours

Ingredients:

- 1 pound pork stew meat, cubed
- 1 red onion, sliced
- 1 carrot, sliced
- 1 teaspoon sweet paprika
- ½ teaspoon cumin, ground
- 1 cup tomato paste
- 1 cup veggie stock
- 2 tablespoons chili powder
- 2 teaspoons cayenne pepper
- 1 tablespoon red pepper flakes
- A pinch of salt and black pepper
- 1 red bell pepper, chopped
- 1 yellow bell pepper, chopped
- 1 tablespoon chives, chopped

Directions:

1. In your Crock Pot, mix the pork meat with the onion, carrot and the other ingredients, toss, put the lid on and cook on Low for 10 hours.
2. Divide the mix into bowls and serve.

Nutrition Info:

- calories 261, fat 7, fiber 4, carbs 8, protein 18

Indian Chickpea Curry

Servings: 8

Cooking Time: 8 1/4 Hours

Ingredients:

- 1 1/2 cups dried chickpeas
- 2 cups butternut squash cubes
- 1/2 teaspoon chili powder
- 1 teaspoon curry powder
- 1/2 teaspoon garam masala

- 2 tablespoons tomato paste
- 1/2 cup tomato sauce
- 1/2 teaspoon cumin powder
- 1/2 teaspoon dried oregano
- 2 cups vegetable stock
- 1 cup coconut milk
- 1 stalk lemongrass, crushed
- 1 bay leaf
- 2 kaffir lime leaves
- Salt and pepper to taste
- 1 lime, juiced
- 2 tablespoons chopped cilantro

Directions:

1. Combine all the ingredients in a crock pot.
2. Add salt and pepper to taste and cook on low settings for 8 hours.
3. Serve the curry warm, topped with chopped cilantro and lime juice.

Black Eyed Peas And Okra Stew

Servings: 8

Cooking Time: 6 1/4 Hours

Ingredients:

- 2 cups dried black eyes peas, rinsed
- 2 cups water
- 1 cup tomato sauce
- 2 large onions, chopped
- 2 cups chopped okra
- 2 red bell peppers, cored and diced
- 1 celery stalk, sliced
- 1 jalapeno peppers, chopped
- Salt and pepper to taste

Directions:

1. Combine all the ingredients in your crock pot.
2. Add salt and pepper to taste and cook on low settings for 6 hours.
3. Serve the dish warm and fresh.

Farro Pumpkin Stew

Servings: 6

Cooking Time: 6 1/4 Hours

Ingredients:

- 2 tablespoons butter
- 1 cup farro, rinsed
- 2 cups pumpkin cubes
- 1 shallot, chopped
- 1 garlic clove, minced
- 1/4 teaspoon cumin seeds
- 1/4 teaspoon fennel seeds
- 1/4 cup white wine
- 2 1/2 cups vegetable stock
- Salt and pepper to taste
- 1/2 cup grated Parmesan cheese

Directions:

1. Combine the butter, faro, pumpkin, shallot, garlic, cumin seeds, fennel seeds, wine and stock in your crock pot.
2. Add salt and pepper to taste and cook on low settings for 6 hours.
3. Serve the stew warm or chilled.

Coffee Beef Roast

Servings: 6

Cooking Time: 4 1/4 Hours

Ingredients:

- 2 pounds beef sirloin
- 2 tablespoons olive oil
- 4 garlic cloves, minced
- 1 cup strong brewed coffee
- 1/2 cup beef stock
- Salt and pepper to taste

Directions:

1. Combine all the ingredients in your crock pot, adding salt and pepper to taste.
2. Cover with a lid and cook on high settings for 4 hours.
3. Serve the roast warm and fresh with your favorite side dish.

Poultry Recipes

Poultry Recipes

Fennel And Chicken Saute

Servings:4

Cooking Time: 7 Hours

Ingredients:

- 1 cup fennel, peeled, chopped
- 10 oz chicken fillet, chopped
- 1 tablespoon tomato paste
- 1 cup of water
- 1 teaspoon ground black pepper
- 1 teaspoon olive oil
- ½ teaspoon fennel seeds

Directions:

1. Heat the olive oil in the skillet.
2. Add fennel seeds and roast them until you get saturated fennel smell.
3. Transfer the seeds in the Crock Pot.
4. Add fennel, chicken fillet, tomato paste, water, and ground black pepper.
5. Close the lid and cook the meal on Low for 7 hours.

Nutrition Info:

- Per Serving: 157 calories, 28.1g protein, 2.8g carbohydrates, 6.5g fat, 1.1g fiber, 63mg cholesterol, 78mg sodium, 314mg potassium.

Lemony Chicken

Servings: 6

Cooking Time: 4 Hours

Ingredients:

- 1 whole chicken, cut into medium pieces
- Salt and black pepper to the taste
- Zest of 2 lemons

- Juice of 2 lemons
- Lemon rinds from 2 lemons

Directions:

1. Put chicken pieces in your Crock Pot, season with salt and pepper to the taste, drizzle lemon juice, add lemon zest and lemon rinds, cover and cook on High for 4 hours.
2. Discard lemon rinds, divide chicken between plates, drizzle sauce from the Crock Pot over it and serve.

Nutrition Info:

- calories 334, fat 24, fiber 2, carbs 4.5, protein 27

Turkey And Carrots

Servings: 2

Cooking Time: 7 Hours

Ingredients:

- 1 pound turkey breasts, skinless, boneless and cubed
- 1 cup carrots, peeled and sliced
- 2 tablespoons avocado oil
- 1 tablespoon balsamic vinegar
- 2 scallions, chopped
- 1 teaspoon turmeric powder
- 1 cup chicken stock
- ½ cup chives, chopped

Directions:

1. In your Crock Pot, mix the turkey with the carrots, oil, vinegar and the other ingredients, toss, put the lid on and cook on Low for 7 hours.
2. Divide the mix between plates and serve right away.

Nutrition Info:

- calories 210, fat 8, fiber 2, carbs 6, protein 11

Chicken Thighs And Mushrooms

Servings: 4

Cooking Time: 4 Hours

Ingredients:

- 4 chicken thighs
- 2 cups mushrooms, sliced
- ¼ cup butter, melted
- Salt and black pepper to the taste
- ½ teaspoon onion powder
- ½ teaspoon garlic powder
- ½ cup water
- 1 teaspoon Dijon mustard
- 1 tablespoon tarragon, chopped

Directions:

1. In your Crock Pot, mix chicken with butter, mushrooms, salt, pepper, onion powder, garlic powder, water, mustard and tarragon, toss, cover and cook on High for 4 hours.
2. Divide between plates and serve.

Nutrition Info:

- calories 453, fat 32, fiber 6, carbs 15, protein 36

Thai Peanut Chicken

Servings: 8

Cooking Time: 4 Hours

Ingredients:

- 2 and ½ pounds chicken thighs and drumsticks
- 1 tablespoon soy sauce
- 1 tablespoon apple cider vinegar
- A pinch of red pepper flakes
- Salt and black pepper to the taste
- ½ teaspoon ginger, ground
- 1/3 cup peanut butter
- 1 garlic clove, minced
- ½ cup warm water

Directions:

1. In your blender mix peanut butter with water, soy sauce, salt, pepper, pepper flakes, ginger, garlic and vinegar and blend well.
2. Pat dry chicken pieces, arrange them in your Crock Pot, cover and cook on High for 4 hours.
3. Divide between plates and serve.

Nutrition Info:

- calories 375, fat 12, fiber 1, carbs 10, protein 42

Goose With Mushroom Cream

Servings: 5

Cooking Time: 5 Hours

Ingredients:

- 1 goose breast, Total Fat: trimmed off and cut into pieces
- 1 goose leg, skinless
- 1 goose thigh, skinless
- Salt and black pepper to the taste
- 3 and ½ cups of water
- 2 tsp garlic, minced
- 1 yellow onion, chopped
- 12 oz. canned mushroom cream

Directions:

1. Add good breast, leg, thigh, and all other ingredients to the Crock Pot.
2. Put the cooker's lid on and set the cooking time to 5 hours on Low settings.
3. Serve warm.

Nutrition Info:

- Per Serving: Calories: 272, Total Fat: 4g, Fiber: 7g, Total Carbs: 16g, Protein: 22g

Lemon Sauce Dipped Chicken

Servings: 11

Cooking Time: 7 Hours

Ingredients:

- 23 oz. chicken breast, boneless, diced
- 1 lemon, juiced and zest
- 1 tbsp cornstarch
- 1 tsp salt
- 1 cup heavy cream
- 1 tbsp flour
- 1 tsp ground black pepper
- 1 tsp minced garlic
- 1 tbsp mustard
- 3 tbsp lemon juice
- 1 red onion, chopped

Directions:

1. Mix lemon juice with salt, garlic, and black pepper in a bowl.
2. Toss in chicken bread, and onion then mix well. Marinate this chicken for 15 minutes.
3. Transfer the marinated chicken along with lemon marinade to the Crock Pot.
4. Put the cooker's lid on and set the cooking time to 3 hours on High settings.
5. Whisk cream with flour, cornstarch, and mustard in a bowl.
6. Cook this cream mixture in a skillet for 10 minutes then transfer to the Crock Pot.
7. Put the cooker's lid on and set the cooking time to 4 hours on Low settings.
8. Serve warm.

Nutrition Info:

- Per Serving: Calories: 154, Total Fat: 9.6g, Fiber: 0g, Total Carbs: 3.59g, Protein: 13g

Goose And Sauce

Servings: 4

Cooking Time: 5 Hours

Ingredients:

- 1 goose breast half, skinless, boneless and cut into thin slices
- ¼ cup olive oil
- 1 sweet onion, chopped
- 2 teaspoons garlic, chopped
- Salt and black pepper to the taste
- ¼ cup sweet chili sauce

Directions:

1. In your Crock Pot, mix goose with oil, onion, garlic, salt, pepper and chili sauce, stir, cover and cook on Low for 5 hours.
2. Divide between plates and serve.

Nutrition Info:

- calories 192, fat 4, fiber 8, carbs 12, protein 22

Duck Breast And Veggies

Servings: 2

Cooking Time: 4 Hours

Ingredients:

- 2 duck breasts, skin on and thinly sliced
- 2 zucchinis, sliced
- 1 tablespoon olive oil
- 1 spring onion stack, chopped
- 1 radish, chopped
- 2 green bell peppers, chopped
- Salt and black pepper to the taste

Directions:

1. In your Crock Pot, mix duck with oil, salt and pepper and toss.
2. Add zucchinis, onion, radish and bell peppers, cover and cook on High for 4 hours.
3. Divide everything between plates and serve.

Nutrition Info:

- calories 450, fat 23, fiber 3, carbs 14, protein 50

Rotisserie Chicken

Servings: 4

Cooking Time: 3 Hours

Ingredients:

- Cooking spray
- 1 tablespoons smoked paprika
- 2 tablespoons brown sugar
- 1 tablespoon chili powder
- 1 teaspoon thyme, chopped
- 1 whole chicken
- Salt and black pepper to the taste

Directions:

1. In a bowl, mix smoked paprika with sugar, chili powder, thyme, salt and pepper, stir and rub the chicken with this mix.
2. Grease the Crock Pot with cooking spray, line it with tin foil, add chicken, cover and cook on High for 3 hours and 30 minutes.
3. Serve right away.

Nutrition Info:

- calories 324, fat 4, fiber 7, carbs 16, protein 3

Cauliflower Chicken

Servings:6

Cooking Time: 7 Hours

Ingredients:

- 2 cups cauliflower, chopped
- 1-pound ground chicken
- 1 teaspoon chili powder
- 1 teaspoon ground turmeric
- 1 teaspoon salt
- 1 cup of water
- 3 tablespoons plain yogurt

Directions:

1. Mix ground chicken with chili powder, ground turmer-

ic, and salt.
2. Then mix the chicken mixture with cauliflower and transfer in the Crock Pot.
3. Add plain yogurt and water.
4. Close the lid and cook the meal on Low for 7 hours.

Nutrition Info:

- Per Serving: 160 calories, 23.1g protein, 2.8g carbohydrates, 5.8g fat, 1.1g fiber, 68mg cholesterol, 473mg sodium, 320mg potassium.

Herbed Chicken Salsa

Servings: 4

Cooking Time: 7 Hrs

Ingredients:

- 4 chicken breasts, skinless and boneless
- ½ cup veggie stock
- Salt and black pepper to the taste
- 16 oz. salsa
- 1 and ½ tbsp parsley, dried
- 1 tsp garlic powder
- ½ tbsp cilantro, chopped
- 1 tsp onion powder
- ½ tbsp oregano, dried
- ½ tsp paprika, smoked
- 1 tsp chili powder
- ½ tsp cumin, ground

Directions:

1. Add chicken breasts, salsa, and all other ingredients to the Crock Pot.
2. Put the cooker's lid on and set the cooking time to 7 hours on Low settings.
3. Serve the chicken with its sauce on top.
4. Devour.

Nutrition Info:

- Per Serving: Calories 270, Total Fat 4g, Fiber 2g, Total Carbs 14g, Protein 9g

Green Chicken Salad

Servings: 4

Cooking Time: 3.5 Hours

Ingredients:

- 1 cup celery stalk, chopped
- 10 oz chicken fillet
- 1 teaspoon salt
- 1 teaspoon ground black pepper
- 1 cup of water
- 1 tablespoon mustard
- 1 tablespoon mayonnaise
- 1 teaspoon lemon juice
- 1 cup arugula, chopped
- 1 cup of green grapes

Directions:

1. Put the chicken in the Crock Pot.
2. Add salt and ground black pepper. Add water.
3. Cook the chicken in high for 5 hours.
4. Meanwhile, put green grapes, arugula, and celery stalk in the bowl.
5. Then chopped the cooked chicken and add it in the arugula mixture.
6. In the shallow bowl, mix mustard with lemon juice, and mayonnaise.
7. Add the mixture in the salad and shake it well.

Nutrition Info:

- Per Serving: 184 calories, 21.7g protein, 7.1g carbohydrates, 7.5g fat, 1.3g fiber, 64mg cholesterol, 693mg sodium, 329mg potassium.

Braised Chicken With Bay Leaf

Servings: 4

Cooking Time: 8 Hours

Ingredients:

- 1-pound chicken breast, skinless

- 1 teaspoon salt
- 4 bay leaves
- 1 teaspoon garlic powder
- 3 cups of water

Directions:

1. Put all ingredients in the Crock Pot and close the lid.
2. Cook the chicken on low for 8 hours.
3. Then chop the chicken and transfer in the bowls.
4. Add chicken liquid from the Crock Pot.

Nutrition Info:

- Per Serving: 135 calories, 24.2g protein, 1.3g carbohydrates, 2.9g fat, 0.3g fiber, 73mg cholesterol, 645mg sodium, 434mg potassium.

Harissa Chicken Breasts

Servings: 6

Cooking Time: 8 Hours

Ingredients:

- 1 tablespoon olive oil
- 1-pound chicken breasts, skin and bones removed
- Salt to taste
- 2 tablespoon Harissa or Sriracha sauce
- 2 tablespoons toasted sesame seeds

Directions:

1. Pour oil in the crockpot.
2. Arrange the chicken breasts and season with salt and pepper to taste
3. Stir in the Sriracha or Harissa sauce. Give a good stir to incorporate everything.
4. Close the lid and cook on low for 8 hours or on high for 6 hours.
5. Once cooked, sprinkle toasted sesame seeds on top.

Nutrition Info:

- Calories per serving: 167; Carbohydrates: 1.1g; Protein: 16.3g; Fat: 10.6g; Sugar: 0g; Sodium: 632mg; Fiber: 0.6g

Citrus Chicken

Servings: 4

Cooking Time: 4 Hours

Ingredients:

- 2 pounds chicken thighs, skinless, boneless and cut into pieces
- Salt and black pepper to the taste
- 3 tablespoons olive oil
- ¼ cup flour
- For the sauce:
- 2 tablespoons fish sauce
- 1 and ½ teaspoons orange extract
- 1 tablespoon ginger, grated
- ¼ cup orange juice
- 2 teaspoons sugar
- 1 tablespoon orange zest
- ¼ teaspoon sesame seeds
- 2 tablespoons scallions, chopped
- ½ teaspoon coriander, ground
- 1 cup water
- ¼ teaspoon red pepper flakes
- 2 tablespoons soy sauce

Directions:

1. In a bowl, mix flour and salt and pepper, stir, add chicken pieces and toss to coat well.
2. Heat up a pan with the oil over medium heat, add chicken, cook until they are golden on both sides and transfer to your Crock Pot.
3. In your blender, mix orange juice with ginger, fish sauce, soy sauce, stevia, orange extract, water and coriander and blend well.
4. Pour this over the chicken, sesame seeds, orange zest, scallions and pepper flakes, stir, cover and cook on High for 4 hours.
5. Divide between plates and serve.

Nutrition Info:

- calories 423, fat 20, fiber 5, carbs 12, protein 45

Chicken Pocket

Servings:4

Cooking Time: 4 Hours

Ingredients:

- 1-pound chicken fillet, skinless, boneless
- 3 oz prunes, chopped
- 1 teaspoon dried cilantro
- 1 tablespoon olive oil
- 1 teaspoon salt
- ½ cup of water

Directions:

1. Make the horizontal cut in the chicken fillet and fill it with prunes.
2. Then secure the cut and rub the chicken fillet with dried cilantro and salt.
3. Sprinkle the chicken with olive oil and transfer in the Crock Pot.
4. Add water and close the lid.
5. Cook the chicken on High for 4 hours.
6. Drain water and remove the toothpicks.
7. Cut the cooked meal into 4 servings.

Nutrition Info:

- Per Serving: 297 calories, 33.3g protein, 13.6g carbohydrates, 12g fat, 1.5g fiber, 101mg cholesterol, 680mg sodium, 432mg potassium.

Chicken Sausages In Jam

Servings:4

Cooking Time: 6 Hours

Ingredients:

- ½ cup of strawberry jam
- ½ cup of water
- 1-pound chicken breast, skinless, boneless, chopped
- 1 teaspoon white pepper

Directions:

1. Sprinkle the chicken meat with white pepper and put it in the Crock Pot.
2. Then mix jam with water and pour the liquid over the chicken.
3. Close the lid and cook it on Low for 6 hours.

Nutrition Info:

- Per Serving: 282 calories, 24.1g protein, 37.5g carbohydrates, 2.9g fat, 0.1g fiber, 73mg cholesterol, 59mg sodium, 427mg potassium.

Vinegar Chicken Wings

Servings:8

Cooking Time: 3 Hours

Ingredients:

- ½ cup apple cider vinegar
- 1 teaspoon garlic powder
- 1 teaspoon smoked paprika
- ½ cup plain yogurt
- 3-pounds chicken wings

Directions:

1. Mix plain yogurt with smoked paprika, garlic powder, and apple cider vinegar.
2. Pour the liquid in the Crock Pot.
3. Add chicken wings and close the lid.

4. Cook the meal on High for 3 hours.

Nutrition Info:

- Per Serving: 339 calories, 50.2g protein, 1.6g carbohydrates, 12.8g fat, 0.1g fiber, 152mg cholesterol, 158mg sodium, 470mg potassium.

Turkey Chili

Servings: 2

Cooking Time: 5 Hours

Ingredients:

- 1 pound turkey breast, skinless, boneless and cubed
- 1 red chili, minced
- 1 teaspoon chili powder
- 1 red onion, chopped
- 1 tablespoon avocado oil
- ½ cup tomato passata
- ½ cup chicken stock
- A pinch of salt and black pepper
- 1 tablespoon cilantro, chopped

Directions:

1. In your Crock Pot, mix the turkey with the chili, chili powder and the other ingredients, toss, put the lid on and cook on High for 5 hours.
2. Divide the mix into bowls and serve.

Nutrition Info:

- calories 263, fat 12, fiber 2, carbs 7, protein 18

Beef, Pork & Lamb Recipes

Beef, Pork & Lamb Recipes

Sweet Pork Shoulder

Servings:2

Cooking Time: 8 Hours

Ingredients:

- 8 oz pork shoulder
- 3 tablespoons agave syrup
- 1 tablespoon sunflower oil
- ½ cup of water

Directions:

1. Brush the pork shoulder with sunflower oil and agave syrup.
2. Put it in the Crock Pot. Add water.
3. Cook the meat on low for 8 hours.

Nutrition Info:

- Per Serving: 489 calories, 26.4g protein, 25.2g carbohydrates, 31.3g fat, 0g fiber, 102mg cholesterol, 100mg sodium, 393mg potassium

White Beef Chili

Servings:4

Cooking Time: 5 Hours

Ingredients:

- 1 cup white beans, soaked
- 4 cups of water
- ½ cup plain yogurt
- 1 teaspoon chili powder
- 1 teaspoon ground black pepper
- 1 teaspoon salt
- 12 oz ground beef
- 1 onion, diced

Directions:

1. Pour water in the Crock Pot.
2. Add white beans, chili powder, ground black pepper, salt, and ground beef.
3. Then add diced onion and close the lid.
4. Cook the meal on High for 4 hours.
5. Then add plain yogurt, carefully mix the meal, and cook it on High for 1 hour more.

Nutrition Info:

- Per Serving: 362 calories, 39.8g protein, 35.9g carbohydrates, 6.3g fat, 8.6g fiber, 78mg cholesterol, 678mg sodium, 1381mg potassium.

Pork Roast With Apples

Servings:4

Cooking Time: 8 Hours

Ingredients:

- 1-pound pork shoulder, boneless
- 1 teaspoon brown sugar
- 1 teaspoon allspices
- 1 teaspoon thyme
- 1 cup apples, chopped
- 1 yellow onion, sliced
- 2 cups of water

Directions:

1. Sprinkle the pork shoulder with allspices, thyme, and brown sugar. Transfer it in the Crock Pot.
2. Add all remaining ingredients and close the lid.
3. Cook the pork roast on Low for 8 hours.

Nutrition Info:

- Per Serving: 376 calories, 26.9g protein, 11.5g carbohydrates, 24.5g fat, 2.1g fiber, 102mg cholesterol, 83mg sodium, 482mg potassium

Pork Chops Pineapple Satay

Servings: 4

Cooking Time: 6 Hrs.

Ingredients:

- 2 lbs. pork chops
- 1/3 cup sugar
- ¼ cup ketchup
- 15 oz. pineapple, cubed
- 3 tbsp apple cider vinegar
- 5 tbsp soy sauce
- 2 tsp garlic, minced
- 3 tbsp flour

Directions:

1. Whisk ketchup with sugar, soy sauce, vinegar, and tapioca in a large bowl.
2. Add pork chops to the ketchup mixture and mix well to coat.
3. Transfer the pork along with ketchup marinade to the insert of Crock Pot.
4. Add garlic and pineapple to the chops.
5. Put the cooker's lid on and set the cooking time to 6 hours on Low settings.
6. Serve warm.

Nutrition Info:

- Per Serving: Calories: 345, Total Fat: 5g, Fiber: 6g, Total Carbs: 13g, Protein: 14g

Lamb Meatballs

Servings:4

Cooking Time: 4 Hours

Ingredients:

- 2 tablespoons minced onion
- 9 oz lamb fillet, minced
- 1 teaspoon Italian seasonings
- 1 teaspoon flour
- 1 tablespoon olive oil
- ½ teaspoon salt
- ½ cup of water

Directions:

1. In the bowl mix minced lamb, minced onion, Italian seasonings, flour, and salt.
2. Make the small meatballs.
3. After this, preheat the olive oil in the skillet.
4. Add meatballs and roast them on high heat for 30 seconds per side.
5. Then transfer the meatballs in the Crock Pot.
6. Add water and cook the meal on high for 4 hours.

Nutrition Info:

- Per Serving: 157 calories, 18g protein, 1.1g carbohydrates, 8.6g fat, 0.1g fiber, 58mg cholesterol, 341mg sodium, 223mg potassium.

Fennel Seeds Pork Chops

Servings:4

Cooking Time: 6 Hours

Ingredients:

- 4 pork chops
- 1 tablespoon fennel seeds
- 3 tablespoons avocado oil
- 1 teaspoon garlic, diced
- ½ cup of water

Directions:

1. Mix fennel seeds with avocado oil and garlic. Mash the mixture.
2. Then rub the pork chops with fennel seeds mixture and transfer in the Crock Pot.
3. Add water and close the lid.
4. Cook the meat on low for 6 hours.

Nutrition Info:

- Per Serving: 276 calories, 18.4g protein, 1.6g carbohydrates, 21.4g fat, 1.1g fiber, 69mg cholesterol, 59mg sodium, 336mg potassium

Spicy Beef Curry

Servings: 6

Cooking Time: 10 Hours

Ingredients:

- 2 ½ pounds beef chuck, cubed
- 1 onion, chopped
- 2 tablespoons curry powder
- 3 cloves of garlic, minced
- ½-inch ginger, grated
- 2 cups coconut milk, unsweetened
- Salt and pepper to taste

Directions:

1. Place all ingredients in the CrockPot.
2. Close the lid and cook on high for 8 hours or on low for 10 hours.

Nutrition Info:

- Calories per serving: 455; Carbohydrates:4.5 g; Protein: 41.3g; Fat: 30.2g; Sugar: 0g; Sodium: 729mg; Fiber: 2.6g

Spiced Pork Belly

Servings: 8

Cooking Time: 12 Hours

Ingredients:

- 1 tablespoon olive oil
- 2-pound pork belly
- 3 cloves of garlic, crushed
- ½ teaspoon ground black pepper
- ½ teaspoon turmeric
- ½ teaspoon ground cumin
- ½ tablespoon lemon juice
- ½ tablespoon salt

Directions:

1. Line the bottom of the CrockPot with aluminum foil. Grease the foil with olive oil.
2. Place all ingredients in a mixing bowl. Massage and allow to marinate in the fridge for 2 hours.
3. Place inside the CrockPot.
4. Close the lid and cook on high for 10 hours or on low for 12 hours.

Nutrition Info:

- Calories per serving: 606; Carbohydrates: 0.9g; Protein: 30.8g; Fat: 29.3g; Sugar: 0g; Sodium: 1007mg; Fiber: 0.4g

Beef With Spinach

Servings: 2

Cooking Time: 7 Hours

Ingredients:

- 1 red onion, sliced
- 1 pound beef stew meat, cubed
- 1 cup tomato passata
- 1 cup baby spinach
- 1 teaspoon olive oil
- Salt and black pepper to the taste
- ½ cup bee stock
- 1 tablespoon basil, chopped

Directions:

1. In your Crock Pot, mix the beef with the onion, passata and the other ingredients except the spinach, toss, put the lid on and cook on Low for 6 hours and 30 minutes.
2. Add the spinach, toss, put the lid on, cook on Low for 30 minutes more, divide into bowls and serve.

Nutrition Info:

- calories 400, fat 15, fiber 4, carbs 25, protein 14

Classic Pork Adobo

Servings: 6

Cooking Time: 12 Hours

Ingredients:

- 2 pounds pork chops, sliced
- 4 cloves of garlic, minced
- 1 onion, chopped
- 2 bay leaves
- ¼ cup soy sauce
- ½ cup lemon juice, freshly squeezed
- 4 quail eggs, boiled and peeled

Directions:

1. Place all ingredients except the quail eggs in the CrockPot.
2. Give a good stir.
3. Close the lid and cook on high for 10 hours or on low for 12 hours.
4. Add in quail eggs an hour before the cooking time ends.

Nutrition Info:

- Calories per serving: 371; Carbohydrates: 6.4g; Protein: 40.7g; Fat: 24.1g; Sugar: 0g; Sodium: 720mg; Fiber: 3.9g

Spicy Indian Beef Roast

Servings: 8

Cooking Time: 10 Hours

Ingredients:

- 2 red onions, chopped
- 2 tablespoon coconut oil
- 1 teaspoon black mustard seed
- 2 ½ pounds grass-fed beef roast
- 25 curry leaves
- 2 tablespoons lemon juice, freshly squeezed
- 4 cloves of garlic, minced

- 1 ½-inch ginger, minced
- 1 serrano pepper, minced
- 1 tablespoon meat masala

Directions:

1. Place all ingredients in the CrockPot.
2. Give a good stir.
3. Close the lid and cook on high for 6 hours or on low for 10 hours.

Nutrition Info:

- Calories per serving: 222; Carbohydrates: 1.1g; Protein: 31.3g; Fat:10.4 g; Sugar: 0g; Sodium: 544mg; Fiber: 0.5g

Lamb With Mint

Servings: 4

Cooking Time: 10 Hours

Ingredients:

- 2 tablespoons ghee
- 1 lamb leg, bone in
- 4 cloves of garlic, minced
- ¼ cup fresh mint, chopped
- ½ teaspoon salt
- A dash of ground black pepper

Directions:

1. Heat oil in skillet over medium flame.
2. Sear the lamb leg for at least 3 minutes on each side.
3. Place in the CrockPot and add the rest of the ingredients.
4. Close the lid and cook on high for 8 hours or on low for 8 hours.

Nutrition Info:

- Calories per serving: 525; Carbohydrates: 6.5g; Protein: 37.4g; Fat: 18.3g; Sugar:0g; Sodium: 748mg; Fiber: 2.4g

Crockpot Beef Picadillo

Servings:8

Cooking Time: 10 Hours

Ingredients:

- 2 pounds ground beef
- 1 ½ tablespoons chili powder
- 2 tablespoon dried oregano
- 1 teaspoon cinnamon powder
- 1 cup tomatoes, chopped
- 1 red onions, chopped
- 2 Anaheim peppers, seeded and chopped
- 20 green olives, pitted and chopped
- 8 cloves of garlic, minced
- Salt and pepper to taste

Directions:

1. Place all ingredients in the CrockPot.
2. Give a good stir.
3. Close the lid and cook on high for 8 hours or on low for 10 hours.

Nutrition Info:

- Calories per serving: 317; Carbohydrates: 4.5g; Protein: 29.6g; Fat: 19.8g; Sugar: 0g; Sodium: 862mg; Fiber: 2.7g

Smoke Infused Lamb

Servings: 4

Cooking Time: 7 Hrs.

Ingredients:

- 4 lamb chops
- 1 tsp liquid smoke
- 1 cup green onions, chopped
- 2 cups canned tomatoes, chopped
- 1 tsp smoked paprika
- 2 tbsp garlic, minced
- Salt and black pepper to the taste

- 3 cups beef stock

Directions:

1. Add lamb, liquid smoke, and all other ingredients to the insert of Crock Pot.
2. Put the cooker's lid on and set the cooking time to 7 hours on Low settings.
3. Serve warm.

Nutrition Info:

- Per Serving: Calories: 364, Total Fat: 12g, Fiber: 7g, Total Carbs: 29g, Protein: 28g

Ketchup Pork Ribs

Servings:4

Cooking Time: 4 Hours

Ingredients:

- 1-pound pork ribs, roughly chopped
- 4 tablespoons ketchup
- 1 tablespoon fresh dill
- 1 tablespoon avocado oil
- ½ cup beef broth

Directions:

1. Mix pork ribs with ketchup and avocado oil.
2. Put them in the Crock Pot.
3. Add beef broth and dill.
4. Close the pork ribs on High for 4 hours.

Nutrition Info:

- Per Serving: 336 calories, 31.1g protein, 4.5g carbohydrates, 20.8g fat, 0.3g fiber, 117mg cholesterol, 330mg sodium, 447mg potassium

Thai Spiced Pork

Servings: 4

Cooking Time: 7 Hrs.

Ingredients:

- 2 tbsp olive oil
- 2 lbs. pork butt, boneless and cubed
- Salt and black pepper to the taste
- 6 eggs, hard-boiled, peeled and sliced
- 1 tbsp cilantro, chopped
- 1 tbsp coriander seeds
- 1 tbsp ginger, grated
- 1 tbsp black peppercorns
- 2 tbsp garlic, chopped
- 2 tbsp five-spice powder
- 1 and ½ cup of soy sauce
- 2 tbsp cocoa powder
- 1 yellow onion, chopped
- 8 cups of water

Directions:

1. Mix pork with salt, peppercorns, and all other ingredients to the insert of Crock Pot.
2. Put the cooker's lid on and set the cooking time to 7 hours on Low settings.
3. Serve warm.

Nutrition Info:

- Per Serving: Calories: 400, Total Fat: 10g, Fiber: 9g, Total Carbs: 28g, Protein: 22g

Simple Roast Beef

Servings:4

Cooking Time: 12 Hours

Ingredients:

- 2 pounds rump roast
- 1 cup onion, chopped
- 3 tablespoons butter

- Salt and pepper to taste
- ¼ cup water

Directions:

1. Place all ingredients in the crockpot.
2. Give a good stir.
3. Close the lid and cook on low for 12 hours or on high for 10 hours.
4. Once cooked, shred the pot roast using two forks.
5. Return to the crockpot and continue cooking on high for 1 hour.

Nutrition Info:

- Calories per serving: 523; Carbohydrates:1.8g; Protein: 43.6g; Fat: 32.6g; Sugar: 0g; Sodium: 734mg; Fiber:1.2 g

Bbq Beer Beef Tenderloin

Servings:4

Cooking Time: 10 Hours

Ingredients:

- ¼ cup beer
- 1-pound beef tenderloin
- ½ cup BBQ sauce
- 1 teaspoon fennel seeds
- 1 teaspoon olive oil

Directions:

1. Mix BBQ sauce with beer, fennel seeds, and olive oil.
2. Pour the liquid in the Crock Pot.
3. Add beef tenderloin and close the lid.
4. Cook the meal on Low for 10 hours.

Nutrition Info:

- Per Serving: 299 calories, 33g protein, 12.1g carbohydrates, 11.7g fat, 0.4g fiber, 104mg cholesterol, 418mg sodium, 482mg potassium.

Short Ribs

Servings: 6

Cooking Time: 10 Hours

Ingredients:

- 3 pounds beef short ribs
- 1 fennel bulb, cut into wedges
- 2 yellow onions, cut into wedges
- 1 cup carrot, sliced
- 14 ounces canned tomatoes, chopped
- 1 cup dry red wine
- 2 tablespoons tapioca, crushed
- 2 tablespoons tomato paste
- 1 teaspoon rosemary, dried
- Salt and black pepper to the taste
- 4 garlic cloves, minced

Directions:

1. In your Crock Pot, mix short ribs with fennel, onions, carrots, tomatoes, wine, tapioca, tomato paste, salt, pepper, rosemary and garlic, cover and cook on Low for 10 hours.
2. Divide everything between plates and serve.

Nutrition Info:

- calories 432, fat 14, fiber 6, carbs 25, protein 42

Cider Dipped Pork Roast

Servings: 6

Cooking Time: 8 Hrs.

Ingredients:

- 1 yellow onion, chopped
- 2 tbsp sweet paprika
- 15 oz. canned tomato, roasted and chopped
- 1 tsp cumin, ground
- 1 tsp coconut oil
- Salt and black pepper to the taste
- A pinch of nutmeg, ground
- 5 lbs. pork roast
- Juice of 1 lemon
- ¼ cup apple cider vinegar

Directions:

1. Place a suitable pan over medium-high heat and add oil.
2. Toss in onions and sauté for few minutes until brown.
3. Transfer the onion to your Crock Pot then add paprika and remaining ingredients.
4. Put the cooker's lid on and set the cooking time to 8 hours on Low settings.
5. Slice the meat and serve warm with its sauce.
6. Enjoy.

Nutrition Info:

- Per Serving: Calories: 350, Total Fat: 5g, Fiber: 2g, Total Carbs: 13g, Protein: 24g

Fish & Seafood Recipes

Fish & Seafood Recipes

Chili Perch

Servings:4

Cooking Time: 3 Hours

Ingredients:

- 1 chili pepper, chopped
- 1 carrot, grated
- 1 onion, diced
- 1 tablespoon coconut oil
- 1 teaspoon salt
- ½ cup chicken stock
- 1-pound perch fillet, chopped

Directions:

1. Put the chili pepper in the Crock Pot.
2. Add carrot, onion, and coconut oil.
3. Sprinkle the perch fillet with salt and transfer in the Crock Pot.
4. Add chicken stock and close the lid.
5. Cook the perch on High for 3 hours.

Nutrition Info:

- Per Serving: 159 calories, 21.6g protein, 4.3g carbohydrates, 5.6g fat, 1g fiber, 45mg cholesterol, 779mg sodium, 93mg potassium

Thai Salmon Cakes

Servings: 10

Cooking Time: 6 Hrs.

Ingredients:

- 6 oz squid, minced
- 10 oz salmon fillet, minced
- 2 tbsp chili paste
- 1 tsp cayenne pepper
- 2 oz lemon leaves
- 3 tbsp green peas, mashed
- 2 tsp fish sauce
- 2 egg white
- 1 egg yolk
- 1 tsp oyster sauce
- 1 tsp salt
- ½ tsp ground coriander
- 1 tsp sugar
- 2 tbsp butter
- ¼ cup cream
- 3 tbsp almond flour

Directions:

1. Mix seafood with chili paste, cayenne pepper, lemon leaves, mashed green peas, fish sauce, whisked egg yolk and egg whites in a bowl.
2. Stir in sugar, salt, oyster sauce, sugar, almond flour, and ground coriander.
3. Mix well, then make small-sized fish cakes out of this mixture.
4. Add cream and butter to the insert of the Crock Pot.
5. Place the fish cakes in the butter and cream.
6. Put the cooker's lid on and set the cooking time to 5 hours on Low settings.
7. Serve warm with cream mixture.

Nutrition Info:

- Per Serving: Calories: 112, Total Fat: 6.7g, Fiber: 1g, Total Carbs: 2.95g, Protein: 10g

Lemon Scallops

Servings: 4

Cooking Time: 1 Hour

Ingredients:

- 1-pound scallops
- 1 teaspoon salt
- 1 teaspoon ground white pepper
- ½ teaspoon olive oil
- 3 tablespoons lemon juice
- 1 teaspoon lemon zest, grated
- 1 tablespoon dried oregano
- ½ cup of water

Directions:

1. Sprinkle the scallops with salt, ground white pepper, lemon juice, and lemon zest and leave for 10-15 minutes to marinate.
2. After this, sprinkle the scallops with olive oil and dried oregano.
3. Put the scallops in the Crock Pot and add water.
4. Cook the seafood on High for 1 hour.

Nutrition Info:

- Per Serving: 113 calories, 19.3g protein, 4.1g carbohydrates, 1.7g fat, 0.7g fiber, 37mg cholesterol, 768mg sodium, 407mg potassium

Spiced Mackerel

Servings: 4

Cooking Time: 4 Hours

Ingredients:

- 1-pound mackerel, peeled, cleaned
- 1 teaspoon salt
- 1 teaspoon ground black pepper
- ½ teaspoon ground clove
- 1 cup of water
- 1 tablespoon olive oil

Directions:

1. Sprinkle the fish with salt, ground black pepper, ground clove, and olive oil.
2. Then put the fish in the Crock Pot. Add water.
3. Close the lid and cook the mackerel on high for 4 hours.

Nutrition Info:

- Per Serving: 329 calories, 27.1g protein, 0.5g carbohydrates, 23.8g fat, 0.2g fiber, 85mg cholesterol, 678mg sodium, 465mg potassium.

Crockpot Manhattan-style Clam Chowder

Servings: 4

Cooking Time: 3 Hours

Ingredients:

- 1 cup onion, chopped
- 2 cups nitrate-free bacon
- 3 ribs of celery, chopped
- 1 tablespoon parsley, chopped
- 1 ½ cups tomatoes, crushed
- 1 bay leaf
- 1 teaspoon dried thyme
- 2 cups diced clams, drained
- 1 can clam juice
- 1 tablespoon melted butter
- Salt and pepper to taste

Directions:

1. Place all ingredients in the CrockPot.
2. Give a good stir.
3. Close the lid and cook on high for 2 hours or on low for 3 hours.
4. Garnish with chopped parsley if desired.

Nutrition Info:

- Calories per serving: 365; Carbohydrates: 6.3g; Protein: 34.1g; Fat: 28.4g; Sugar: 0.5g; Sodium: 728mg; Fiber: 4.3g

Haddock Chowder

Servings: 5

Cooking Time: 6 Hours

Ingredients:

- 1-pound haddock, chopped
- 2 bacon slices, chopped, cooked
- ½ cup potatoes, chopped
- 1 teaspoon ground coriander
- ½ cup heavy cream
- 4 cups of water
- 1 teaspoon salt

Directions:

1. Put all ingredients in the Crock Pot and close the lid.
2. Cook the chowder on Low for 6 hours.

Nutrition Info:

- Per Serving: 203 calories, 27.1g protein, 2.8g carbohydrates, 8.6g fat, 0.4g fiber, 97mg cholesterol, 737mg sodium, 506mg potassium

Poached Cod And Pineapple Mix

Servings: 2

Cooking Time: 4 Hours

Ingredients:

- 1 pound cod, boneless
- 6 garlic cloves, minced
- 1 small ginger pieces, chopped
- ½ tablespoon black peppercorns
- 1 cup pineapple juice
- 1 cup pineapple, chopped
- ¼ cup white vinegar
- 4 jalapeno peppers, chopped
- Salt and black pepper to the taste

Directions:

1. Put the fish in your crock, season with salt and pepper.
2. Add garlic, ginger, peppercorns, pineapple juice, pineapple chunks, vinegar and jalapenos.
3. Stir gently, cover and cook on Low for 4 hours.
4. Divide fish between plates, top with the pineapple mix and serve.

Nutrition Info:

- calories 240, fat 4, fiber 4, carbs 14, protein 10

Salmon Salad

Servings: 2

Cooking Time: 3 Hours

Ingredients:

- 1 pound salmon fillets, boneless and cubed
- ¼ cup chicken stock
- 1 zucchini, cut with a spiralizer
- 1 carrot, sliced
- 1 eggplant, cubed
- ½ cup cherry tomatoes, halved
- 1 red onion, sliced
- ½ teaspoon turmeric powder
- ½ teaspoon chili powder
- ½ tablespoon rosemary, chopped
- A pinch of salt and black pepper
- 1 tablespoon chives, chopped

Directions:

1. In your Crock Pot, mix the salmon with the zucchini, stock, carrot and the other ingredients,, toss , put the lid on and cook on High for 3 hours.
2. Divide the mix into bowls and serve.

Nutrition Info:

- calories 424, fat 15.1, fiber 12.4, carbs 28.1, protein 49

Sage Shrimps

Servings:4

Cooking Time: 1 Hour

Ingredients:

- 1-pound shrimps, peeled
- 1 teaspoon dried sage
- 1 teaspoon minced garlic
- 1 teaspoon white pepper
- 1 cup tomatoes chopped
- ½ cup of water

Directions:

1. Put all ingredients in the Crock Pot and close the lid.
2. Cook the shrimps on High for 1 hour.

Nutrition Info:

- Per Serving: 146 calories, 26.4g protein, 4.1g carbohydrates, 2.1g fat, 0.8g fiber, 239mg cholesterol, 280mg sodium, 310mg potassium.

Semolina Fish Balls

Servings: 11

Cooking Time: 8 Hrs.

Ingredients:

- 1 cup sweet corn
- 5 tbsp fresh dill, chopped
- 1 tbsp minced garlic
- 7 tbsp bread crumbs
- 2 eggs, beaten
- 10 oz salmon, salmon
- 2 tbsp semolina
- 2 tbsp canola oil
- 1 tsp salt
- 1 tsp ground black pepper
- 1 tsp cumin
- 1 tsp lemon zest
- ¼ tsp cinnamon
- 3 tbsp almond flour
- 3 tbsp scallion, chopped

- 3 tbsp water

Directions:

1. Mix sweet corn, dill, garlic, semolina, eggs, salt, cumin, almond flour, scallion, cinnamon, lemon zest, and black pepper in a large bowl.
2. Stir in chopped salmon and mix well.
3. Make small meatballs out of this fish mixture then roll them in the breadcrumbs.
4. Place the coated fish ball in the insert of the Crock Pot.
5. Add canola oil and water to the fish balls.
6. Put the cooker's lid on and set the cooking time to 8 hours on Low settings.
7. Serve warm.

Nutrition Info:

- Per Serving: Calories: 201, Total Fat: 7.9g, Fiber: 2g, Total Carbs: 22.6g, Protein: 11g

Shrimp And Cauliflower Bowls

Servings: 2

Cooking Time: 2 Hours

Ingredients:

- 1 pound shrimp, peeled and deveined
- ½ cup chicken stock
- 1 cup cauliflower florets
- ½ teaspoon turmeric powder
- ½ teaspoon coriander, ground
- ½ cup tomato passata
- A pinch of salt and black pepper
- 1 tablespoon cilantro, chopped

Directions:

1. In your Crock Pot, mix the cauliflower with the stock, turmeric and the other ingredients except the shrimp, toss, put the lid on and cook on High for 1 hour.
2. Add the shrimp, toss, cook on High for 1 more hour, divide into bowls and serve.

Nutrition Info:

- calories 232, fat 9, fiber 2, carbs 6, protein 8

Nutmeg Trout

Servings:4

Cooking Time: 3 Hours

Ingredients:

- 1 tablespoon ground nutmeg
- 1 tablespoon butter, softened
- 1 teaspoon dried cilantro
- 1 teaspoon dried oregano
- 1 teaspoon fish sauce
- 4 trout fillets
- ½ cup of water

Directions:

1. In the shallow bowl mix butter with cilantro, dried oregano, and fish sauce. Add ground nutmeg and whisk the mixture.
2. Then grease the fish fillets with nutmeg mixture and put in the Crock Pot.
3. Add remaining butter mixture and water.
4. Cook the fish on high for 3 hours.

Nutrition Info:

- Per Serving: 154 calories, 16.8g protein, 1.2g carbo-hydrates, 8.8g fat, 0.5g fiber, 54mg cholesterol, 178mg sodium, 305mg potassium.

Paprika Cod

Servings: 2

Cooking Time: 3 Hours

Ingredients:

- 1 tablespoon olive oil
- 1 pound cod fillets, boneless
- 1 teaspoon sweet paprika
- ¼ cup chicken stock
- ¼ cup white wine
- 2 scallions, chopped
- ½ teaspoon rosemary, dried
- A pinch of salt and black pepper

Directions:

1. In your Crock Pot, mix the cod with the paprika, oil and the other ingredients, toss gently, put the lid on and cook on High for 3 hours.
2. Divide everything between plates and serve.

Nutrition Info:

- calories 211, fat 8, fiber 4, carbs 8, protein 8

Cod With Asparagus

Servings: 4

Cooking Time: 2 Hrs

Ingredients:

- 4 cod fillets, boneless
- 1 bunch asparagus
- 12 tbsp lemon juice
- Salt and black pepper to the taste
- 2 tbsp olive oil

Directions:

1. Place the cod fillets in separate foil sheets.
2. Top the fish with asparagus spears, lemon pepper, oil, and lemon juice.
3. Wrap the fish with its foil sheet then place them in Crock Pot.
4. Put the cooker's lid on and set the cooking time to 2 hours on High settings.
5. Unwrap the fish and serve warm.

Nutrition Info:

- Per Serving: Calories 202, Total Fat 3g, Fiber 6g, Total Carbs 7g, Protein 3g

Miso Cod

Servings:4

Cooking Time: 4 Hours

Ingredients:

- 1-pound cod fillet, sliced
- 1 teaspoon miso paste
- ½ teaspoon ground ginger
- 2 cups chicken stock
- ½ teaspoon ground nutmeg

Directions:

1. In the mixing bowl mix chicken stock, ground nutmeg, ground ginger, and miso paste.
2. Then pour the liquid in the Crock Pot.
3. Add cod fillet and close the lid.
4. Cook the fish on Low for 4 hours.

Nutrition Info:

- Per Serving: 101 calories, 20.8g protein, 1.1g carbohydrates, 1.5g fat, 0.2g fiber, 56mg cholesterol, 506mg sodium, 14mg potassium.

Rice Stuffed Trout

Servings: 5

Cooking Time: 4 Hrs.

Ingredients:

- 16 oz whole trout, peeled
- ½ cup sweet corn
- ¼ cup of rice, cooked
- 1 sweet pepper, chopped
- 1 tbsp salt
- 1 tsp thyme
- 1 tsp ground black pepper
- ½ tsp paprika
- 1 tbsp olive oil
- 1 tbsp sour cream
- ¼ cup cream cheese
- 3 lemon wedges
- 2 tbsp chives

Directions:

1. Mix sweet corn, cooked rice, and sweet pepper in a suitable bowl.
2. Whisk chives, salt, sour cream, olive oil, cream cheese, paprika, thyme, black pepper in a separate bowl.
3. Place the trout fish in a foil sheet and brush it with a cream cheese mixture.
4. Stuff the fish with rice mixture and top the fish with lemon wedges.
5. Wrap the stuffed with the foil sheet.
6. Put the cooker's lid on and set the cooking time to 4 hours on High settings.
7. Serve warm.

Nutrition Info:

- Per Serving: Calories: 255, Total Fat: 13.9g, Fiber: 2g, Total Carbs: 13.57g, Protein: 22g

Salmon Stew

Servings: 6

Cooking Time: 5 Hours 15 Minutes

Ingredients:

- 2 tablespoons butter
- 2 pounds salmon fillet, cubed
- 2 medium onions, chopped
- Salt and black pepper, to taste
- 2 cups homemade fish broth

Directions:

1. Put all the ingredients in the one pot crock pot and thoroughly mix.
2. Cover and cook on LOW for about 5 hours.
3. Dish out and serve hot.

Nutrition Info:

- Calories: 293 Fat: 8.7g Carbohydrates: 16.3g

Chinese Cod

Servings: 4

Cooking Time: 2 Hours

Ingredients:

- 1 pound cod, cut into medium pieces
- Salt and black pepper to the taste
- 2 green onions, chopped
- 3 garlic cloves, minced
- 3 tablespoons soy sauce
- 1 cup fish stock
- 1 tablespoons balsamic vinegar
- 1 tablespoon ginger, grated
- ½ teaspoon chili pepper, crushed

Directions:

1. In your Crock Pot, mix fish with salt, pepper green onions, garlic, soy sauce, fish stock, vinegar, ginger and chili pepper, toss, cover and cook on High for 2 hours.
2. Divide everything between plates and serve.

Nutrition Info:

- calories 204, fat 3, fiber 6, carbs 14, protein 24

Cod And Peas

Servings: 4

Cooking Time: 2 Hours

Ingredients:

- 16 ounces cod fillets
- 1 tablespoon parsley, chopped
- 10 ounces peas
- 9 ounces wine
- ½ teaspoon oregano, dried
- ½ teaspoon paprika
- 2 garlic cloves, chopped
- Salt and pepper to the taste

Directions:

1. In your food processor mix garlic with parsley, oregano, paprika and wine, blend well and add to your Crock Pot.
2. Add fish, peas, salt and pepper, cover and cook on High for 2 hours.
3. Divide into bowls and serve.

Nutrition Info:

- calories 251, far 2, fiber 6, carbs 7, protein 22

Salmon And Berries

Servings: 2

Cooking Time: 3 Hours

Ingredients:

- 1 pound salmon fillets, boneless and roughly cubed
- ½ cup blackberries
- Juice of 1 lime
- 1 tablespoon avocado oil
- 2 scallions, chopped
- ½ teaspoon Italian seasoning
- ½ cup fish stock
- A pinch of salt and black pepper

Directions:

1. In your Crock Pot, mix the salmon with the berries, lime juice and the other ingredients, toss, put the lid on and cook on Low for 3 hours.
2. Divide the mix between plates and serve.

Nutrition Info:

- calories 211, fat 13, fiber 2, carbs 7, protein 11

Soups & Stews Recipes

Soups & Stews Recipes

Chicken Bacon Orzo Soup

Servings: 6 (1.7 Ounces Per Serving)

Cooking Time: 5 Hours

Ingredients:

- 5 slices of bacon
- 2 cups yellow onion, diced
- 2 cloves garlic, minced
- 1 cup carrots, diced
- 1 cup celery, diced
- 6 cups chicken stock
- ½ cup orzo
- 1 ½ teaspoons sea salt
- ½ teaspoon fresh ground pepper
- Parsley, fresh, chopped to taste

Directions:

1. Cook bacon in pan over medium-high heat until crisp. Place bacon on plate lined with paper towels. Save 2 tablespoons of fat from pan. Add the garlic, celery, carrots, onions to the pan with a pinch of salt. Cook the veggies over medium heat for several minutes, stirring periodically. Place chicken breasts in Crock-Pot and cover with veggies and chicken stock. Cover and cook over LOW heat for 5 hours. Halfway through cooking time, take out chicken, shred it up, and then place back in Crock-Pot along with orzo. Garnish each bowl of soup with diced bacon and fresh parsley. Serve hot.

Nutrition Info:

- Calories: 507, Total Fat: 7 g, Saturated Fat: 1 g, Sodium: 220 mg, Carbs: 87 g, Fiber: 23 g, Sugars: 10 g, Protein: 28.3 g

Shrimp Soup

Servings: 6

Cooking Time: 6 1/4 Hours

Ingredients:

- 2 tablespoons olive oil
- 1 large sweet onion, chopped
- 1 fennel bulb, sliced
- 4 garlic cloves, chopped
- 1 cup dry white wine
- 1/2 cup tomato sauce
- 2 cup water
- 1 teaspoon dried oregano
- 1 teaspoon dried basil
- 1 pinch chili powder
- 4 medium size tomatoes, peeled and diced
- 1 bay leaf
- 1/2 pound cod fillets, cubed
- 1/2 pound fresh shrimps, peeled and deveined
- Salt and pepper to taste
- 1 lime, juiced

Directions:

1. Heat the oil in a skillet and stir in the onion, fennel and garlic. Sauté for 5 minutes until softened.
2. Transfer the mixture in your Crock Pot and stir in the wine, tomato sauce, water, oregano, basil, chili powder, tomatoes and bay leaf.
3. Cook on high settings for 1 hour then add the cod and shrimps, as well as lime juice, salt and pepper and continue cooking on low settings for 5 additional hours.
4. Serve the soup warm or chilled.

Jamaican Stew

Servings:8

Cooking Time: 1 Hour

Ingredients:

- 1 tablespoon coconut oil
- 1 teaspoon garlic powder
- ½ cup bell pepper, sliced
- ½ cup heavy cream
- 1-pound salmon fillet, chopped
- 1 teaspoon ground coriander
- ½ teaspoon ground cumin

Directions:

1. Put the coconut oil in the Crock Pot.
2. Then mix the salmon with ground cumin and ground coriander and put in the Crock Pot.
3. Add the layer of bell pepper and sprinkle with garlic powder.
4. Add heavy cream and close the lid.
5. Cook the stew on High for 1 hour.

Nutrition Info:

- Per Serving: 120 calories, 11.3g protein, 1.1g carbohydrates, 8g fat, 6.9g fiber, 35mg cholesterol, 28mg sodium, 244mg potassium.

Creamy Carrot Lentil Soup

Servings: 6

Cooking Time: 2 1/4 Hours

Ingredients:

- 2 tablespoons olive oil
- 4 carrots, sliced
- 1 shallot, chopped
- 1 small fennel bulb, sliced
- 1/2 cup red lentils
- 2 cups chicken stock
- 2 cups water

- 1/4 teaspoon cumin powder
- Salt and pepper to taste
- 1 thyme sprig
- 1 rosemary sprig

Directions:

1. Heat the oil in a skillet and add the shallot and carrots. Sauté for 5 minutes then transfer the mixture in your Crock Pot.
2. Add the remaining ingredients and cook on high settings for 2 hours.
3. When done, remove the thyme and rosemary and puree the soup with an immersion blender.
4. Serve the soup warm.

Cream Of Broccoli Soup

Servings: 6

Cooking Time: 2 1/4 Hours

Ingredients:

- 2 shallots, chopped
- 2 garlic cloves, chopped
- 2 tablespoons olive oil
- 1 head broccoli, cut into florets
- 2 potatoes, peeled and cubed
- 1 cup chicken stock
- 2 cups water
- Salt and pepper to taste
- 1/2 teaspoon dried basil
- 1/2 teaspoon dried oregano

Directions:

1. Heat the oil in a skillet and stir in the shallots and garlic. Sauté for a few minutes until softened then transfer in your Crock Pot.
2. Add the broccoli, potatoes, chicken stock and water, as well as dried herbs, salt and pepper.
3. Cook on high settings for 2 hours then puree the soup in a blender until creamy and rich.
4. Pour the soup into bowls in order to serve.

Grits Potato Soup

Servings: 6

Cooking Time: 6 1/4 Hours

Ingredients:

- 4 bacon slices, chopped
- 1/2 cup grits
- 2 cups chicken stock
- 4 cups water
- 1 1/2 pounds potatoes, peeled and cubed
- 1/2 celery stalk, sliced
- 1 carrot, diced
- 1 parsnip, diced
- 1 cup diced tomatoes
- 1/2 teaspoon dried thyme
- 1/2 teaspoon dried oregano
- Salt and pepper to taste

Directions:

1. Cook the bacon until crisp in a skillet or pan.
2. Transfer in your Crock Pot and add the remaining ingredients.
3. Cook the soup on low settings, adjusting the taste with salt and pepper as needed.
4. The soup is done in about 6 hours.
5. Serve warm.

Coconut Cod Stew

Servings:6

Cooking Time: 6.5 Hours

Ingredients:

- 1-pound cod fillet, chopped
- 2 oz scallions, roughly chopped
- 1 cup coconut cream
- 1 teaspoon curry powder
- 1 teaspoon garlic, diced

Directions:

1. Mix curry powder with coconut cream and garlic.
2. Add scallions and gently stir the liquid.
3. After this, pour it in the Crock Pot and add cod fillet.
4. Stir the stew mixture gently and close the lid.
5. Cook the stew on low for 6.5 hours.

Nutrition Info:

- Per Serving: 158 calories, 14.7g protein, 3.3g carbohydrates, 10.3g fat, 1.3g fiber, 37mg cholesterol, 55mg sodium, 138mg potassium.

Green Peas Chowder

Servings:6

Cooking Time: 8 Hours

Ingredients:

- 1-pound chicken breast, skinless, boneless, chopped
- 6 cups of water
- 1 cup green peas
- ¼ cup Greek Yogurt
- 1 tablespoon dried basil
- 1 teaspoon ground black pepper
- ½ teaspoon salt

Directions:

1. Mix salt, chicken breast, ground black pepper, and dried basil.
2. Transfer the ingredients in the Crock Pot.
3. Add water, green peas, yogurt, and close the lid.
4. Cook the chowder on Low for 8 hours.

Nutrition Info:

- Per Serving: 113 calories, 18.2g protein, 4.1g carbohydrates, 2.2g fat, 1.3g fiber, 49mg cholesterol, 244mg sodium, 359mg potassium.

Salmon Fennel Soup

Servings: 6

Cooking Time: 5 1/4 Hours

Ingredients:

- 1 shallot, chopped
- 1 garlic clove, sliced
- 1 fennel bulb, sliced
- 1 carrot, diced
- 1 celery stalk, sliced
- 3 salmon fillets, cubed
- 1 lemon, juiced
- 1 bay leaf
- Salt and pepper to taste

Directions:

1. Combine the shallot, garlic, fennel, carrot, celery, fish, lemon juice and bay leaf in your Crock Pot.
2. Add salt and pepper to taste and cook on low settings for 5 hours.
3. Serve the soup warm.

Hamburger Soup

Servings: 8

Cooking Time: 7 Hours 15 Minutes

Ingredients:

- 1 pound ground meat, cooked
- 1 can diced tomatoes
- 1 can lima beans
- Salt, to taste
- 2 tablespoons olive oil
- 1 can kidney beans
- 1 can mixed vegetables
- 1½ teaspoons red chili powder
- 1 can beef broth

Directions:

1. Put olive oil and ground meat in a crock pot and cook

for about 5 minutes.
2. Transfer the remaining ingredients into the crock pot and cover the lid.
3. Cook on LOW for about 7 hours and ladle out into serving bowl to serve hot.

Nutrition Info:

- Calories: 262 Fat: 14.4g Carbohydrates: 12.2g

Posole Soup

Servings: 8

Cooking Time: 6 1/4 Hours

Ingredients:

- 1 tablespoons canola oil
- 1 pound pork tenderloin, cubed
- 1 sweet onion, chopped
- 2 garlic cloves, chopped
- 1/2 teaspoon cumin powder
- 1/2 teaspoon dried oregano
- 1/2 teaspoon dried basil
- 1/4 teaspoon chili powder
- 1 can (15 oz.) black beans, drained
- 1 can sweet corn, drained
- 1 cup diced tomatoes
- 2 jalapeno peppers, chopped
- 4 cups chicken stock
- 2 cups water
- Salt and pepper to taste
- 2 limes, juiced

Directions:

1. Heat the canola oil in a skillet and stir in the tenderloin. Cook for 5 minutes on all sides.
2. Add the pork in your Crock Pot and stir in the remaining ingredients, except the lime juice.
3. Add salt and pepper to taste and cook on low settings for 6 hours.
4. When done, stir in the lime juice and serve the soup warm or chilled.

Mexican Beef Soup

Servings: 6

Cooking Time: 8 1/4 Hours

Ingredients:

- 1 pound ground beef
- 2 tablespoons canola oil
- 2 red bell peppers, cored and diced
- 1 sweet onion, chopped
- 2 cups beef stock
- 1 can (15 oz.) diced tomatoes
- 1 can (15 oz.) black beans, drained
- 3 cups water
- 1/2 cup red salsa
- 1 chipotle pepper, chopped
- Salt and pepper to taste

Directions:

1. Heat the oil in a skillet and stir in the beef. Cook for 5 minutes, stirring often, then transfer the beef in your Crock Pot.
2. Add the remaining ingredients and adjust the taste with salt and pepper.
3. Cook on low settings for 8 hours.
4. Serve the soup warm or chilled.

Lamb Stew

Servings:5

Cooking Time: 5 Hours

Ingredients:

- 1 pound lamb meat, cubed
- 1 red onion, sliced
- 1 teaspoon cayenne pepper
- 1 teaspoon dried rosemary
- ½ teaspoon dried thyme
- 1 cup potatoes, chopped
- 4 cups of water

Directions:

1. Sprinkle the lamb meat with cayenne pepper, dried rosemary, and dried thyme.
2. Transfer the meat in the Crock Pot.
3. Add water, onion, and potatoes.
4. Close the lid and cook the stew on high for 5 hours.

Nutrition Info:

- Per Serving: 216 calories, 17.7g protein, 7.2g carbohydrates, 12.2g fat, 1.4g fiber, 64mg cholesterol, 73mg sodium, 166mg potassium.

Curried Prawn Soup

Servings: 6

Cooking Time: 6 1/4 Hours

Ingredients:

- 2 tablespoons olive oil
- 2 shallots, chopped
- 1 carrot, sliced
- 1/2 head cauliflower, cut into florets
- 2 cups cherry tomatoes, halved
- 2 cups chicken stock
- 4 cups water
- 2 tablespoons lemon juice
- 1 tablespoon red curry paste
- Salt and pepper to taste
- 1 pound fresh shrimps, peeled and deveined

Directions:

1. Combine the olive oil, shallots, carrot, cauliflower and tomatoes in your Crock Pot.
2. Add the stock, water, curry paste and lemon juice and season with salt and pepper.
3. Place the shrimps on top and cook on high settings for 2 hours.
4. Serve the soup warm.

Smoked Sausage Stew

Servings:5

Cooking Time: 3.5 Hours

Ingredients:

- 1-pound smoked sausages, chopped
- 1 cup broccoli, chopped
- 1 cup tomato juice
- 1 cup of water
- 1 teaspoon butter
- 1 teaspoon dried thyme
- ¼ cup Cheddar cheese, shredded

Directions:

1. Grease the Crock Pot bowl with butter from inside.
2. Put the smoked sausages in one layer in the Crock Pot.
3. Add the layer of broccoli and Cheddar cheese.
4. Then mix water with tomato juice and dried thyme.
5. Pour the liquid over the sausage mixture and close the lid.
6. Cook the stew on high for 3.5 hours.

Nutrition Info:

- Per Serving: 352 calories, 20g protein, 3.5g carbohydrates, 28.5g fat, 0.7g fiber, 84mg cholesterol, 858mg sodium, 443mg potassium

Bacon Potato Soup

Servings: 8

Cooking Time: 6 1/2 Hours

Ingredients:

- 1 cup diced bacon
- 1 sweet onion, chopped
- 1 garlic clove, chopped
- 1 carrot, diced
- 1 celery stalk, sliced
- 2 pounds potatoes, peeled and cubed
- 2 cups chicken stock

- 4 cups water
- Salt and pepper to taste
- 1/4 teaspoon cumin seeds

Directions:

1. Heat a skillet over medium flame and add the bacon. Cook until golden on all sides and transfer in your Crock Pot.
2. Add the remaining ingredients and season with salt and pepper.
3. Cook on low settings for 6 hours.
4. Serve the soup warm.

Chicken Parmesan Soup

Servings: 8

Cooking Time: 8 1/4 Hours

Ingredients:

- 8 chicken thighs
- 1 sweet onion, chopped
- 1 celery stalk, sliced
- 1 carrot, sliced
- 1 celery root, peeled and cubed
- 2 large potatoes, peeled and cubed
- 1 can diced tomatoes
- 2 cups chicken stock
- 6 cups water
- Salt and pepper to taste
- 2 tablespoons chopped parsley
- Parmesan shavings for serving

Directions:

1. Combine the chicken thighs, onion, celery, carrot, celery root, potatoes and tomatoes in your Crock Pot.
2. Add the stock, water, salt and pepper and cook on low settings for 8 hours.
3. When done, stir in the chopped parsley.
4. Serve the soup topped with Parmesan shavings.

Pork And Corn Soup

Servings: 8

Cooking Time: 8 1/4 Hours

Ingredients:

- 1 pound pork roast, cubed
- 1 sweet onion, chopped
- 2 bacon slices, chopped
- 1 garlic clove, chopped
- 2 carrots, sliced
- 1 celery stalk, sliced
- 2 yellow bell peppers, cored and diced
- 2 cups frozen sweet corn
- 1/2 teaspoon cumin seeds
- 1/2 red chili, sliced
- 2 cups chicken stock
- 4 cups water
- Salt and pepper to taste
- 2 tablespoons chopped cilantro

Directions:

1. Combine the pork roast, sweet onion, bacon and garlic in a skillet and cook for 5 minutes, stirring all the time.
2. Transfer in your Crock Pot and add the carrots, celery, bell peppers, sweet corn, cumin seeds, red chili, stock, water, salt and pepper.
3. Cook on low settings for 8 hours.
4. When done, add the chopped cilantro and serve the soup warm.

Corn And Red Pepper Chowder

Servings: 8

Cooking Time: 8 1/4 Hours

Ingredients:

- 2 tablespoons olive oil
- 1 shallot, chopped
- 1 red bell pepper, cored and diced
- 2 large potatoes, peeled and cubed
- 2 cups frozen sweet corn
- 2 cups chicken stock
- 2 cups water
- 1/4 teaspoon smoked paprika
- 1/4 teaspoon cumin powder
- Salt and pepper to taste

Directions:

1. Heat the oil in a skillet and stir in the shallot. Sauté until softened then transfer in your Crock Pot.
2. Add the remaining ingredients and adjust the taste with salt and pepper.
3. Cook on low settings for 8 hours.
4. When done, puree the soup in a blender and serve it warm.

Bean Medley Soup

Servings: 10

Cooking Time: 8 1/2 Hours

Ingredients:

- 2 sweet onions, chopped
- 2 carrots, diced
- 1 celery stalk, sliced
- 1 parsnip, diced
- 2 red bell peppers, cored and diced
- 1/4 cup dried black beans
- 1/4 cup dried kidney beans
- 1/4 cup dried cannellini beans
- 1/2 cup dried white beans
- 1/4 cup dried chickpeas
- 1 can fire roasted tomatoes
- 2 cups chicken stock
- 6 cups water
- 1 bay leaf
- Salt and pepper to taste

Directions:

1. Combine all the ingredients in your Crock Pot.
2. Add salt and pepper to taste and cook on low settings for 8 hours.
3. Serve the soup warm or chilled.

Snack Recipes

Snack Recipes

Spinach Cream Dip

Servings: 8

Cooking Time: 3 Hrs 20 Minutes

Ingredients:

- 2 cups cream cheese
- 2 cups fresh spinach, chopped
- 1 tsp salt
- 1 tsp ground black pepper
- 1 tsp paprika
- 1 tsp ground white pepper
- 7 oz. Mozzarella, cut into strips
- 1 onion, peeled and chopped
- 1 tbsp Tabasco sauce
- 1 tbsp butter
- 3 tbsp milk

Directions:

1. Whisk cream cheese, black pepper, salt, white pepper, paprika, cream cheese, milk, and Tabasco sauce in a bowl.
2. Stir in onion and transfer this mixture to the Crock Pot.
3. Put the cooker's lid on and set the cooking time to 20 minutes on High settings.
4. Stir in spinach and mozzarella strips.
5. Put the cooker's lid on and set the cooking time to 3 hours on High settings.
6. Serve.

Nutrition Info:

- Per Serving: Calories: 241, Total Fat: 18.9g, Fiber: 1g, Total Carbs: 6.03g, Protein: 13g

Crab Dip(1)

Servings: 2

Cooking Time: 1 Hour

Ingredients:

- 2 ounces crabmeat
- 1 tablespoon lime zest, grated
- ½ tablespoon lime juice
- 2 tablespoons mayonnaise
- 2 green onions, chopped
- 2 ounces cream cheese, cubed
- Cooking spray

Directions:

1. Grease your Crock Pot with the cooking spray, and mix the crabmeat with the lime zest, juice and the other ingredients inside.
2. Put the lid on, cook on Low for 1 hour, divide into bowls and serve as a party dip.

Nutrition Info:

- calories 100, fat 3, fiber 2, carbs 9, protein 4

Creamy Mushroom Spread

Servings: 2

Cooking Time: 4 Hours

Ingredients:

- 1 pound mushrooms, sliced
- 3 garlic cloves, minced
- 1 cup heavy cream
- 2 teaspoons smoked paprika
- Salt and black pepper to the taste
- 2 tablespoons parsley, chopped

Directions:

1. In your Crock Pot, mix the mushrooms with the garlic and the other ingredients, whisk, put the lid on and cook on Low for 4 hours.
2. Whisk, divide into bowls and serve as a party spread.

Nutrition Info:

- calories 300, fat 6, fiber 12, carbs 16, protein 6

Cheesy Potato Dip

Servings: 12

Cooking Time: 5 Hours

Ingredients:

- 1 cup heavy cream
- 1 cup milk
- 2 tbsp cornstarch
- 5 medium potatoes, peeled and diced
- 5 oz. Cheddar cheese, chopped
- 1 cup fresh cilantro
- 1 tsp salt
- 1 tsp black pepper
- 1 tsp paprika
- ½ tsp onion powder
- 1 tbsp garlic powder
- ¼ tsp oregano

Directions:

1. Add milk, cream, potatoes, salt, paprika, onion powder, oregano, garlic powder, and black pepper to the Crock Pot.
2. Put the cooker's lid on and set the cooking time to 3 hours on High settings.
3. Stir in cilantro and cheese to the cooked potatoes.
4. Put the cooker's lid on and set the cooking time to 2 hours on High settings.
5. Mix well and serve.

Nutrition Info:

- Per Serving: Calories: 196, Total Fat: 5.6g, Fiber: 4g, Total Carbs: 31.58g, Protein: 6g

Tex Mex Dip

Servings: 6

Cooking Time: 1 Hour

Ingredients:

- 15 ounces canned chili con carne
- 1 cup Mexican cheese, shredded
- 1 yellow onion, chopped
- 8 ounces cream cheese, cubed
- ½ cup beer
- A pinch of salt
- 12 ounces macaroni, cooked
- 1 tablespoons cilantro, chopped

Directions:

1. In your Crock Pot, mix chili con carne with cheese, onion, cream cheese, beer and salt, stir, cover and cook on High for 1 hour.
2. Add macaroni and cilantro, stir, divide into bowls and serve.

Nutrition Info:

- calories 200, fat 4, fiber 6, carbs 17, protein 5

Apple Dip

Servings: 8

Cooking Time: 1 Hour And 30 Minutes

Ingredients:

- 5 apples, peeled and chopped
- ½ teaspoon cinnamon powder
- 12 ounces jarred caramel sauce
- A pinch of nutmeg, ground

Directions:

1. In your Crock Pot, mix apples with cinnamon, caramel sauce and nutmeg, stir, cover and cook on High for 1 hour and 30 minutes.
2. Divide into bowls and serve.

Nutrition Info:

- calories 200, fat 3, fiber 6, carbs 10, protein 5

Artichoke & Spinach Mash

Servings: 8 (5.6 Ounces Per Serving)

Cooking Time: 2 Hours And 25 Minutes

Ingredients:

- 1 ½ cups frozen spinach, thawed
- 2 cans artichoke hearts, drained and chopped
- 1 cup sour cream
- ¾ cup Parmesan cheese, freshly grated
- ½ cup Feta cheese, crumbled
- 1 cup cream cheese
- 2 green onions, diced
- 2 cloves garlic, minced
- ¼ teaspoon ground pepper

Directions:

1. Add artichoke hearts, spinach, and other ingredients to Crock-Pot. Stir until all ingredients are well combined. Top with cream cheese. Cover and cook on LOW for 2 hours and 15 minutes. Before serving, give dish a good stir.

Nutrition Info:

- Calories: 258.99, Total Fat: 20.42 g, Saturated Fat: 11.93 g, Cholesterol: 63.44 mg, Sodium: 436.59 mg, Potassium: 394.51 mg, Total Carbohydrates: 8.45 g Fiber: 4.07 g, Sugar: 2.53 g, Protein: 10 g

Curried Meatballs

Servings: 40

Cooking Time: 4 Hours

Ingredients:

- 12 ounces pineapple preserves
- 8 ounces pineapple tidbits in juice
- 8 ounces Dijon mustard
- ½ cup brown sugar
- 1 teaspoon curry powder
- 2 and ½ pounds frozen meatballs

Directions:

1. In your Crock Pot, mix pineapple preserves with pineapple tidbits, mustard, sugar and curry powder and whisk well.
2. Add meatballs, toss, cover and cook on High for 4 hours.
3. Serve them hot.

Nutrition Info:

- calories 120, fat 5, fiber 1, carbs 13, protein 6

Mozzarella Basil Tomatoes

Servings: 8

Cooking Time: 30 Minutes

Ingredients:

- 3 tbsp fresh basil
- 1 tsp chili flakes
- 5 oz. Mozzarella, sliced
- 4 large tomatoes, sliced
- 1 tbsp olive oil
- 1 tsp minced garlic
- ½ tsp onion powder
- ½ tsp cilantro

Directions:

1. Whisk olive oil with onion powder, cilantro, garlic, and chili flakes in a bowl.
2. Rub all the tomato slices with this cilantro mixture.
3. Top each tomato slice with cheese slice and then place another tomato slice on top to make a sandwich.
4. Insert a toothpick into each tomato sandwich to seal it.
5. Place them in the base of the Crock Pot.
6. Put the cooker's lid on and set the cooking time to 20 minutes on High settings.
7. Garnish with basil.
8. Enjoy.

Nutrition Info:

- Per Serving: Calories: 59, Total Fat: 1.9g, Fiber: 2g, Total Carbs: 4.59g, Protein: 7g

Jalapeno Poppers

Servings: 4

Cooking Time: 3 Hours

Ingredients:

- ½ pound chorizo, chopped
- 10 jalapenos, tops cut off and deseeded
- 1 small white onion, chopped
- ½ pound beef, ground
- ¼ teaspoon garlic powder
- 1 tablespoon maple syrup
- 1 tablespoon mustard
- 1/3 cup water

Directions:

1. In a bowl, mix beef with chorizo, garlic powder and onion and stir.
2. Stuff your jalapenos with the mix, place them in your Crock Pot, add the water, cover and cook on High for 3 hours.
3. Transfer jalapeno poppers to a lined baking sheet.
4. In a bowl, mix maple syrup with mustard, whisk well, brush poppers with this mix, arrange on a platter and serve.

Nutrition Info:

- calories 214, fat 2, fiber 3, carbs 8, protein 3

Chicken Meatballs

Servings: 2

Cooking Time: 7 Hours

Ingredients:

- A pinch of red pepper flakes, crushed
- ½ pound chicken breast, skinless, boneless, ground
- 1 egg, whisked
- ½ cup salsa Verde
- 1 teaspoon oregano, dried
- ½ teaspoon chili powder
- ½ teaspoon rosemary, dried
- 1 tablespoon parsley, chopped
- A pinch of salt and black pepper

Directions:

1. In a bowl, mix the chicken with the egg and the other ingredients except the salsa, stir well and shape medium meatballs out of this mix.
2. Put the meatballs in the Crock Pot, add the salsa Verde, toss gently, put the lid on and cook on Low for 7 hours.
3. Arrange the meatballs on a platter and serve.

Nutrition Info:

- calories 201, fat 4, fiber 5, carbs 8, protein 2

Squash Salsa

Servings: 2

Cooking Time: 3 Hours

Ingredients:

- 1 cup butternut squash, peeled and cubed
- 1 cup cherry tomatoes, cubed
- 1 cup avocado, peeled, pitted and cubed
- ½ tablespoon balsamic vinegar
- ½ tablespoon lemon juice
- 1 tablespoon lemon zest, grated
- ¼ cup veggie stock
- 1 tablespoon chives, chopped
- A pinch of rosemary, dried
- A pinch of sage, dried
- A pinch of salt and black pepper

Directions:

1. In your Crock Pot, mix the squash with the tomatoes, avocado and the other ingredients, toss, put the lid on and cook on Low for 3 hours.
2. Divide into bowls and serve as a snack.

Nutrition Info:

- calories 182, fat 5, fiber 7, carbs 12, protein 5

Broccoli Dip

Servings: 2

Cooking Time: 2 Hours

Ingredients:

- 1 green chili pepper, minced
- 2 tablespoons heavy cream
- 1 cup broccoli florets
- 1 tablespoon mayonnaise
- 2 tablespoons cream cheese, cubed
- A pinch of salt and black pepper
- 1 tablespoon chives, chopped

Directions:

1. In your Crock Pot, mix the broccoli with the chili pepper, mayo and the other ingredients, toss, put the lid on and cook on Low for 2 hours.
2. Blend using an immersion blender, divide into bowls and serve as a party dip.

Nutrition Info:

- calories 202, fat 3, fiber 3, carbs 7, protein 6

Hummus

Servings: 10

Cooking Time: 8 Hours

Ingredients:

- 1 cup chickpeas, dried
- 2 tablespoons olive oil
- 3 cups water
- A pinch of salt and black pepper
- 1 garlic clove, minced
- 1 tablespoon lemon juice

Directions:

1. In your Crock Pot, mix chickpeas with water, salt and pepper, stir, cover and cook on Low for 8 hours.

2. Drain chickpeas, transfer to a blender, add oil, more salt and pepper, garlic and lemon juice, blend well, divide into bowls and serve.

Nutrition Info:

- calories 211, fat 6, fiber 7, carbs 8, protein 4

Mussels Salad

Servings: 4

Cooking Time: 1 Hour

Ingredients:

- 2 pounds mussels, cleaned and scrubbed
- 1 radicchio, cut into thin strips
- 1 white onion, chopped
- 1 pound baby spinach
- ½ cup dry white wine
- 1 garlic clove, crushed
- ½ cup water
- A drizzle of olive oil

Directions:

1. Divide baby spinach and radicchio in salad bowls and leave aside for now.
2. In your Crock Pot, mix mussels with onion, wine, garlic, water and oil, toss, cover and cook on High for 1 hour.
3. Divide mussels on top of spinach and radicchio, add cooking liquid all over and serve.

Nutrition Info:

- calories 59, fat 4, fiber 1, carbs 1, protein 1

Carrot Broccoli Fritters

Servings: 12

Cooking Time: 4 Hrs

Ingredients:

- 2 large carrots, grated
- 4 oz. broccoli, chopped
- 1 tbsp cream cheese
- ¼ cup flour
- 1 tsp salt
- 1 tsp ground black pepper
- 1 tsp paprika
- 1 tsp butter
- 4 tbsp fresh cilantro, chopped
- 1 egg
- 3 oz. celery stalk

Directions:

1. Whisk egg with cream cheese, salt, flour, cilantro, black pepper, and paprika in a bowl.
2. Stir in celery stalk, carrots and broccoli, and mix to well to form a dough.
3. Divide the broccoli dough into 2 or 4 pieces and roll them into fritters.
4. Grease the base of Crock Pot with butter and these fritters inside.
5. Put the cooker's lid on and set the cooking time to 3 hours on High settings.
6. Flip the Crock Pot fritters and again cover to cook for another 1 hour.
7. Serve fresh,

Nutrition Info:

- Per Serving: Calories: 37, Total Fat: 1.6g, Fiber: 1g, Total Carbs: 4.22g, Protein: 2g

Almond Buns

Servings: 6 (1.9 Ounces Per Serving)

Cooking Time: 20 Minutes

Ingredients:

- 3 cups almond flour
- 5 tablespoons butter
- 1 ½ teaspoons sweetener of your choice (optional)
- 2 eggs
- 1 ½ teaspoons baking powder

Directions:

1. In a mixing bowl, combine the dry ingredients. In another bowl, whisk the eggs. Add melted butter to mixture and mix well. Divide almond mixture equally into 6 parts. Grease the bottom of Crock-Pot and place in 6 almond buns. Cover and cook on HIGH for 2 to 2 ½ hours or LOW for 4 to 4 ½ hours. Serve hot.

Nutrition Info:

- Calories: 219.35, Total Fat: 20.7 g, Saturated Fat: 7.32 g, Cholesterol: 87.44 mg, Sodium: 150.31 mg, Potassium: 145.55 mg, Total Carbohydrates: 4.59 g, Fiber: 1.8 g, Sugar: 1.6 g, Protein: 6.09 g

Macadamia Nuts Snack

Servings: 2

Cooking Time: 2 Hours

Ingredients:

- ½ pound macadamia nuts
- 1 tablespoon avocado oil
- ¼ cup water
- ½ tablespoon chili powder
- ½ teaspoon oregano, dried
- ½ teaspoon onion powder

Directions:

1. In your Crock Pot, mix the macadamia nuts with the oil and the other ingredients, toss, put the lid on, cook on Low for 2 hours, divide into bowls and serve as a snack.

Nutrition Info:

- calories 108, fat 3, fiber 2, carbs 9, protein 2

Eggplant Dip

Servings: 4

Cooking Time: 4 Hours And 10 Minutes

Ingredients:

- 1 eggplant
- 1 zucchini, chopped
- 2 tablespoons olive oil
- 2 tablespoons balsamic vinegar
- 1 tablespoon parsley, chopped
- 1 yellow onion, chopped
- 1 celery stick, chopped
- 1 tomato, chopped
- 2 tablespoons tomato paste
- 1 and ½ teaspoons garlic, minced
- A pinch of sea salt
- Black pepper to the taste

Directions:

1. Brush eggplant with the oil, place on preheated grill and cook over medium-high heat for 5 minutes on each side.
2. Leave aside to cool down, chop it and put in your Crock Pot.
3. Also add, zucchini, vinegar, onion, celery, tomato, parsley, tomato paste, garlic, salt and pepper and stir everything.
4. Cover and cook on High for 4 hours.
5. Stir your spread again very well, divide into bowls and serve.

Nutrition Info:

- calories 110, fat 1, fiber 2, carbs 7, protein 5

Bean Dip

Servings: 56

Cooking Time: 3 Hours

Ingredients:

- 16 ounces Mexican cheese
- 5 ounces canned green chilies
- 16 ounces canned refried beans
- 2 pounds tortilla chips
- Cooking spray

Directions:

1. Grease your Crock Pot with cooking spray, line it, add Mexican cheese, green chilies and refried beans, stir, cover and cook on Low for 3 hours.
2. Divide into bowls and serve with tortilla chips on the side.

Nutrition Info:

- calories 120, fat 2, fiber 1, carbs 14, protein 3

Dessert Recipes

Dessert Recipes

Lemony Orange Marmalade

Servings: 8

Cooking Time: 3 Hrs.

Ingredients:

- Juice of 2 lemons
- 3 lbs. sugar
- 1 lb. oranges, peeled and cut into segments
- 1-pint water

Directions:

1. Whisk lemon juice, sugar, water, and oranges in the insert of Crock Pot.
2. Put the cooker's lid on and set the cooking time to 3 hours on High settings.
3. Serve when chilled.

Nutrition Info:

- Per Serving: Calories: 100, Total Fat: 4g, Fiber: 4g, Total Carbs: 12g, Protein: 4g

Tomato Jam

Servings: 2

Cooking Time: 3 Hours

Ingredients:

- ½ pound tomatoes, chopped
- 1 green apple, grated
- 2 tablespoons red wine vinegar
- 4 tablespoons sugar

Directions:

1. In your Crock Pot, mix the tomatoes with the apple and the other ingredients, whisk, put the lid on and cook on Low for 3 hours.
2. Whisk the jam well, blend a bit using an immersion blender, divide into bowls and serve cold.

Nutrition Info:

- calories 70, fat 1, fiber 1, carbs 18, protein 1

Orange Muffins

Servings:4

Cooking Time: 3 Hours

Ingredients:

- 1 egg, beaten
- 1 teaspoon orange zest, grated
- 1 tablespoon butter, melted
- ½ cup of orange juice
- 1 cup flour
- 1 teaspoon baking powder

Directions:

1. Mix egg with orange juice and butter.
2. Then add baking powder and flour. Stir it until you get the smooth butter.
3. Add orange zest and stir the batter with the help of the spoon.
4. Transfer the batter in the muffin molds, filling ½ part of every mold.
5. Then place them in the Crock Pot and close the lid.
6. Cook the muffins on high for 3 hours.

Nutrition Info:

- Per Serving: 171 calories, 4.9g protein, 27.9g carbohydrates, 4.4g fat, 1g fiber, 49mg cholesterol, 38mg sodium, 238mg potassium.

S'mores Cake

Servings:6

Cooking Time: 2 Hours

Ingredients:

- 1 cup chocolate cake mix
- ¼ cup pudding mix
- 3 eggs, beaten
- ¼ cup plain yogurt
- 3 tablespoons butter, melted
- 3 oz marshmallows
- 3 oz graham crackers, crushed
- Cooking spray

Directions:

1. Mix chocolate cake mix with pudding mix.
2. Add eggs, plain yogurt, and butter. Stir it until homogenous.
3. After this, add graham crackers and carefully mix them again.
4. Spray the Crock Pot bottom with cooking spray and put the chocolate mixture inside.
5. Cook it on high for 2 hours.
6. Then add marshmallows and broil the mixture.

Nutrition Info:

- Per Serving: 390 calories, 7.1g protein, 56.7g carbohydrates, 16.4g fat, 1.5g fiber, 98mg cholesterol, 579mg sodium, 219mg potassium.

Chia Muffins

Servings:4

Cooking Time: 2.5 Hours

Ingredients:

- 2 eggs, beaten
- ¼ cup plain yogurt
- 1 teaspoon ground nutmeg
- 1 tablespoon brown sugar
- ½ cup flour
- 1 tablespoon chia seeds
- 1 teaspoon butter, melted

Directions:

1. Mix eggs with plain yogurt, ground nutmeg, brown sugar, flour, and butter.
2. Whisk the mixture until you get a smooth batter.
3. Then add chia seeds and mix the batter with the help of the spoon.
4. Pour the batter in the silicone muffin molds (fill ½ part of every mold).
5. Place the muffins in the Crock Pot.
6. Close the lid and cook them on High for 2.5 hours.

Nutrition Info:

- Per Serving: 136 calories, 5.9g protein, 17.2g carbohydrates, 4.8g fat, 1.8g fiber, 85mg cholesterol, 50mg sodium, 102mg potassium.

Pomegranate And Mango Bowls

Servings: 2

Cooking Time: 3 Hours

Ingredients:

- 2 cups pomegranate seeds
- 1 cup mango, peeled and cubed
- ½ cup heavy cream
- 1 tablespoon lemon juice
- ½ teaspoon vanilla extract
- 2 tablespoons white sugar

Directions:

1. In your Crock Pot, combine the mango with the pomegranate seeds and the other ingredients, toss, put the lid on and cook on Low for 3 hours.
2. Divide into bowls and serve cold.

Nutrition Info:

- calories 162, fat 4, fiber 5, carbs 20, protein 6

Coconut Clouds

Servings:4

Cooking Time: 2.5 Hours

Ingredients:

- 2 egg whites
- 1 cup coconut shred
- 2 tablespoons of sugar powder

Directions:

1. Whisk the egg whites until you get firm peaks.
2. Add sugar powder and coconut shred and carefully mix the mixture.
3. Then line the Crock Pot with baking paper.
4. With the help of the spoon put the small amount of coconut mixture in the Crock Pot to get the cookies in the shape of clouds.
5. Cook them on High for 2.5 hours.

Nutrition Info:

- Per Serving: 246 calories, 3g protein, 12g carbohydrates, 22g fat, 4g fiber, 80mg cholesterol, 40mg sodium, 0mg potassium.

Red Muffins

Servings:8

Cooking Time: 2 Hours

Ingredients:

- 5 oz carrot, grated
- 2 eggs, beaten
- 3 tablespoons coconut oil, softened
- 2 tablespoons cream cheese
- 1 cup flour
- ¼ cup skim milk
- ¼ cup of sugar
- 1 teaspoon baking powder

Directions:

1. In the bowl mix eggs, coconut oil, cream cheese, flour, skim milk, sugar, and baking powder.
2. Carefully stir the mixture until you get a smooth batter.
3. Then add carrot and stir the mixture with the help of the spoon.
4. Pour the batter in the muffin molds (fill ½ part of every mold) and place it in the Crock Pot.
5. Cook the muffins on high for 2 hours.

Nutrition Info:

- Per Serving: 159 calories, 3.6g protein, 20.8g carbohydrates, 7.2g fat, 0.9g fiber, 44mg cholesterol, 40mg sodium, 167mg potassium.

Vanilla Bean Caramel Custard

Servings: 6

Cooking Time: 6 1/4 Hours

Ingredients:

- 1 cup white sugar for melting
- 4 cups whole milk
- 1 cup heavy cream
- 2 egg yolks
- 4 eggs
- 1 tablespoon vanilla bean paste
- 2 tablespoons white sugar

Directions:

1. Caramelize 1 cup of sugar in a thick saucepan until it has an amber color. Pour the caramel in your Crock Pot and swirl to coat the bottom and sides as much as possible.
2. Mix the milk, cream, egg yolks, eggs, vanilla bean paste and sugar in a bowl. Pour this mixture over the caramel.
3. Cover the pot and cook on low settings for 6 hours.
4. Serve the custard chilled.

Cottage Cheese Corners

Servings:3

Cooking Time: 3 Hours

Ingredients:

- 2 tablespoons cottage cheese
- 1 teaspoon sugar
- 1 teaspoon vanilla extract
- 1 egg, beaten
- 3 oz puff pastry
- Cooking spray

Directions:

1. Mix cottage cheese with sugar, vanilla extract, and ½ of the beaten egg.
2. Stir the mixture until smooth.
3. Then roll up the puff pastry and cut it in the shape of squares.
4. Spread every dough square with a cottage cheese mixture.
5. Then wrap them in the shape of corners.
6. Spray the Crock Pot bowl with cooking spray.
7. Put the corners inside and close the lid.
8. Cook them on High for 3 hours.

Nutrition Info:

- Per Serving: 195 calories, 5.2g protein, 14.8g carbohydrates, 12.4g fat, 0.4g fiber, 55mg cholesterol, 130mg sodium, 48mg potassium.

Sticky Cinnamon Rolls

Servings: 8

Cooking Time: 6 1/2 Hours

Ingredients:

- 4 cups all-purpose flour
- 1/2 teaspoon salt
- 1 teaspoon active dry yeast
- 1 1/2 cups warm milk
- 2 eggs
- 1/4 cup melted butter
- 1 cup white sugar
- 1 teaspoon cinnamon powder
- 1 cup light brown sugar

Directions:

1. Mix the flour, salt and yeast in a bowl.
2. Add the warm milk, eggs and melted butter and knead the dough for 10 minutes until elastic and smooth.
3. Cover the bowl and allow the dough to rise for 1 hour.
4. Transfer the dough on a floured working surface and roll it into a thin sheet that has a rectangular shape.
5. Mix the white sugar with cinnamon and spread it over the dough then roll the dough tightly.
6. Carefully cut the roll of dough into thick slices.
7. Spread the brown sugar in your crock pot then arrange the dough rolls in your Crock Pot, with the cut facing up.
8. Cover the pot and cook on low settings for 5 hours.
9. Serve the rolls warm.

Blueberry Preserve

Servings: 8

Cooking Time: 4 1/4 Hours

Ingredients:

- 4 cups fresh or frozen blueberries
- 2 cups white sugar
- 1 tablespoon lemon zest
- 1 cinnamon stick

Directions:

1. Combine all the ingredients in your crock pot.
2. Cover the pot and cook on low settings for 4 hours.
3. When done, pour the preserve into glass jars and cover them with a lid while still hot.

Creamy Lemon Mix

Servings: 4

Cooking Time: 1 Hr.

Ingredients:

- 2 cups heavy cream
- Sugar to the taste
- 2 lemons, peeled and roughly chopped

Directions:

1. Whisk the cream with lemons and sugar to the insert of Crock Pot.
2. Put the cooker's lid on and set the cooking time to 1 hour on Low settings.
3. Serve when chilled.

Nutrition Info:

- Per Serving: Calories: 177, Total Fat: 0g, Fiber: 0g, Total Carbs: 6g, Protein: 1g

Cinnamon Hot Chocolate

Servings: 3

Cooking Time: 2 Hrs.

Ingredients:

- 2 cups of milk
- 6 oz. condensed milk
- ½ cup of chocolate chips
- 1 cup heavy cream, whipped
- 1 tsp cinnamon

Directions:

1. Add milk, condensed milk, cinnamon, heavy cream, chocolate chips to the insert of Crock Pot.
2. Put the cooker's lid on and set the cooking time to 5 hours on Low settings.
3. Serve.

Nutrition Info:

- Per Serving: Calories: 440, Total Fat: 29.7g, Fiber: 1g, Total Carbs: 34.97g, Protein: 10g

Butterscotch Self Saucing Pudding

Servings: 6

Cooking Time: 2 1/4 Hours

Ingredients:

- 1/2 cup butter, melted
- 1 cup whole milk
- 1 teaspoon vanilla extract
- 1 cup white sugar
- 1 1/2 cups all-purpose flour
- 1/4 teaspoon salt
- 2 cups hot water
- 3/4 cup dark brown sugar
- 2 tablespoons golden syrup
- 2 tablespoons butter

Directions:

1. Make the butterscotch sauce by mixing the hot water, brown sugar, golden syrup and 2 tablespoons of butter in a saucepan. Cook over medium flame for 5-6 minutes until thickened then place aside.
2. For the pudding, mix 1/2 cup butter, milk, vanilla, white sugar, flour and salt in a bowl. Pour the batter in a Crock Pot.
3. Drizzle the butterscotch sauce on top and cook on high settings for 2 hours.
4. Serve the pudding slightly warm.

Apple Cobbler

Servings: 2

Cooking Time: 2 Hours

Ingredients:

- 1 cup apples, diced
- 1 teaspoon ground cinnamon
- ½ cup flour
- 2 tablespoons coconut oil
- ½ cup cream

Directions:

1. Mix flour with sugar and coconut oil and knead the dough.
2. Then mix apples with ground cinnamon and place it in the Crock Pot in one layer.
3. Grate the dough over the apples and add cream.
4. Close the lid and cook the cobbler on High for 2 hours.

Nutrition Info:

- Per Serving: 330 calories, 4.1g protein, 42.1g carbohydrates, 17.5g fat, 4.2g fiber, 11mg cholesterol, 21mg sodium, 180mg potassium.

Maple Pears

Servings: 4

Cooking Time: 4 Hours

Ingredients:

- 4 pears, peeled and tops cut off and cored
- 5 cardamom pods
- 2 cups orange juice
- ¼ cup maple syrup
- 1 cinnamon stick
- 1-inch ginger, grated

Directions:

1. Put the pears in your Crock Pot, add cardamom, or-

ange juice, maple syrup, cinnamon and ginger, cover and cook on Low for 4 hours.
2. Divide pears between plates and serve them with the sauce on top.

Nutrition Info:

- calories 200, fat 4, fiber 2, carbs 3, protein 4

Banana Cookies

Servings: 4

Cooking Time: 2 Hours

Ingredients:

- 2 bananas, mashed
- 1 egg, beaten
- 1 cup oatmeal
- 1 teaspoon ground cinnamon
- Cooking spray

Directions:

1. Mix bananas with egg and ground cinnamon.
2. Add oatmeal and whisk the mixture until smooth.
3. Then spray the Crock Pot with cooking spray.
4. Make the cookies from the banana mixture with the help of the spoon and put them in the Crock Pot.
5. Cook the cookies on High for 2 hours.

Nutrition Info:

- Per Serving: 147 calories, 4.7g protein, 27.9g carbohydrates, 2.6g fat, 3.9g fiber, 41mg cholesterol, 17mg sodium, 302mg potassium.

Apples With Raisins

Servings: 4

Cooking Time: 5 Hours

Ingredients:

- 4 big apples
- 4 teaspoons raisins
- 4 teaspoons sugar
- ½ teaspoon ground cinnamon
- ½ cup of water

Directions:

1. Core the apples and fill them with sugar and raisins.
2. Then arrange the apples in the Crock Pot.
3. Sprinkle them with ground cinnamon.
4. Add water and close the lid.
5. Cook the apples on low for 5 hours.

Nutrition Info:

- Per Serving: 141 calories, 0.7g protein, 37.4g carbohydrates, 0.4g fat, 5.7g fiber, 0mg cholesterol, 3mg sodium, 263mg potassium.

White Chocolate Cheesecake Soufflé

Servings: 8

Cooking Time: 2 1/2 Hours

Ingredients:

- 1 1/2 cups white chocolate chips, melted
- 1 1/2 cups cream cheese, softened
- 4 egg yolks
- 1 teaspoon vanilla extract
- 4 egg whites
- 1 pinch salt
- Butter to grease the pot

Directions:

1. Whip the egg whites with a pinch of salt until stiff.
2. Combine the cream cheese, chocolate, egg yolks and vanilla in a bowl.
3. Fold in the whipped egg whites then pour the batter in your Crock Pot.
4. Cook on high settings for 2 hours.
5. The soufflé can be served both warm and chilled.

Date: _____

MY SHOPPING LIST

Measurement Conversions

BASIC KITCHEN CONVERSIONS & EQUIVALENT

DRY MEASUREMENTS CONVERSION CHART

3 TEASPOONS = 1 TABLESPOON = 1/16 CUP

6 TEASPOONS = 2 TABLESPOONS = 1/8 CUP

12 TEASPOONS = 4 TABLESPOONS = 1/4 CUP

24 TEASPOONS = 8 TABLESPOONS = 1/2 CUP

36 TEASPOONS = 12 TABLESPOONS = 3/4 CUP

48 TEASPOONS = 16 TABLESPOONS = 1 CUP

METRIC TO US COOKING CONVERSIONS

OVEN TEMPERATURE

120℃ = 250° F

160℃ = 320° F

180℃ = 350° F

205℃ = 400° F

220℃ = 425° F

OVEN TEMPERATURE

8 FLUID OUNCES = 1 CUP = 1/2 PINT = 1/4 QUART

16 FLUID OUNCES = 2 CUPS = 1 PINT = 1/2 QUART

32 FLUID OUNCES = 4 CUPS = 2 PINTS = 1 QUART = 1/4 GALLON

128 FLUID OUNCES = 16 CUPS = 8 PINTS = 4 QUARTS = 1 GALLON

BAKING IN GRAMS

1 CUP FLOUR = 140 GRAMS

1 CUP SUGAR = 150 GRAMS

1 CUP POWDERED SUGAR = 160 GRAMS

1 CUP HEAVY CREAM = 235 GRAMS

VOLUME

1 MILLILITER = 1/5 TEASPOON

5 ML = 1 TEASPOON

15 ML = 1 TABLESPOON

240 ML = 1 CUP OR 8 FLUID OUNCES

1 LITER = 34 FL. OUNCES

WEIGHT

1 GRAM = .035 OUNCES

100 GRAMS = 3.5 OUNCES

500 GRAMS = 1.1 POUNDS

1 KILOGRAM = 35 OUNCES

US TO METRIC COOKING CONVERSIONS

1/5 TSP = 1 ML

1 TSP = 5 ML

1 TBSP = 15 ML

1 FL OUNCE = 30 ML

1 CUP = 237 ML

1 PINT (2 CUPS) = 473 ML

1 QUART (4 CUPS) = .95 LITER

1 GALLON (16 CUPS) = 3.8 LITERS

1 OZ = 28 GRAMS

1 POUND = 454 GRAMS

BUTTER

1 CUP BUTTER = 2 STICKS = 8 OUNCES = 230 GRAMS = 8 TABLESPOONS

BUTTER

1 CUP = 8 FLUID OUNCES

1 CUP = 16 TABLESPOONS

1 CUP = 48 TEASPOONS

1 CUP = 1/2 PINT

1 CUP = 1/4 QUART

1 CUP = 1/16 GALLON

1 CUP = 240 ML

BAKING PAN CONVERSIONS

1 CUP ALL-PURPOSE FLOUR = 4.5 OZ

1 CUP ROLLED OATS = 3 OZ 1 LARGE EGG = 1.7 OZ

1 CUP BUTTER = 8 OZ

1 CUP MILK = 8 OZ

1 CUP HEAVY CREAM = 8.4 OZ

1 CUP GRANULATED SUGAR = 7.1 OZ

1 CUP PACKED BROWN SUGAR = 7.75 OZ

1 CUP VEGETABLE OIL = 7.7 OZ

1 CUP UNSIFTED POWDERED SUGAR = 4.4 OZ

BAKING PAN CONVERSIONS

9-INCH ROUND CAKE PAN = 12 CUPS

10-INCH TUBE PAN =16 CUPS

11-INCH BUNDT PAN = 12 CUPS

9-INCH SPRINGFORM PAN = 10 CUPS

9 X 5 INCH LOAF PAN = 8 CUPS

9-INCH SQUARE PAN = 8 CUPS

RECIPES

DATE

RECIPES	Salads	Meats	Soups
SERVES	Grains	Seafood	Snack
PREP TIME	Breads	Vegetables	Breakfast
COOK TIME	Appetizers	Desserts	Lunch
FROM THE KITCHEN OF	Main Dishes	Beverages	Dinners

INGREDIENTS

DIRECTIONS

NOTES

SERVING ☆☆☆☆☆

DIFFICULTY ☆☆☆☆☆

OVERALL ☆☆☆☆☆

Recipe ....

From the kicthen of ....

Serves .... Prep time .... Cook time ....

☐ Difficulty   ☐ Easy   ☐ Medium   ☐ Hard

Ingredient

....

....

....

....

....

Directions ....

....

....

....

....

....

....

Appendix : Recipes Index

Printed in Great Britain
by Amazon